Succeed on the Standardized Test

This Book Includes:

- 2 Summative Assessments (SA)
- Additional practice questions
- Detailed answer explanations for every question
- EBSR (Evidence Based Selected Response) questions
  TECR (Technology Enhanced Constructed Response) questions
  PCRs (Prose Constructed Response(s)) questions
- Strategies for building speed and accuracy
- Content aligned with the Common Core State Standards

Plus access to Online Workbooks which include:

- Hundreds of practice questions
- Self-paced learning and personalized score reports
- Instant feedback after completion of the workbook

Complement Classroom Learning All Year

Using the Lumos Study Program, parents and teachers can reinforce the classroom learning experience for children. It creates a collaborative learning platform for students, teachers and parents.

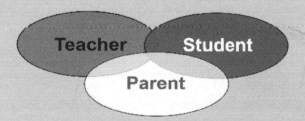

Used in Schools and Public Libraries To Improve Student Achievement

Common Core Assessments and Online Workbooks: Grade 3 Language Arts and Literacy, PARCC Edition

Contributing Editor   -   **Carla G.**
Contributing Editor   -   **Julie Lyons**
Contributing Editor   -   **George Smith**
Contributing Editor   -   **Anneda Nettleton**
Curriculum Director   -   **Marisa Adams**
Executive Producer   -   **Mukunda Krishnaswamy**
Designer and Illustrator -   **Mirona Jova**

ISBN-10: 194048412X

ISBN-13: 978-1-940484-12-9

Printed in the United States of America

For permissions and additional information contact us

Lumos Information Services, LLC
PO Box 1575, Piscataway, NJ 08855-1575
http://www.LumosLearning.com

Email: support@lumoslearning.com
Tel: (732) 384-0146
Fax: (866) 283-6471

Lumos Learning
Developed by Expert Teachers

Table of Contents

Introduction

The Common Core State Standards Initiative (CCSS) was created from the need to have more robust and rigorous guidelines, which could be standardized from state to state. These guidelines create a learning environment where students will be able to graduate high school with all skills necessary to be active and successful members of society, whether they take a role in the workforce or in some sort of post-secondary education.

Once the CCSS were fully developed and implemented, it became necessary to devise a way to ensure they were assessed appropriately. To this end, states adopting the CCSS have joined one of two consortia, either PARCC or Smarter Balanced.

What is PARCC?

The Partnership for Assessment of Readiness and College and Careers (PARCC) is one of the two state consortiums responsible for developing assessments aligned to the new, more rigorous Common Core State Standards. A combination of educational leaders from PARCC Governing and Participating states, along with test developers, have worked together to create the new computer based English Language Arts and Math Assessments.

PARCC's first round of testing occurred during the 2014-2015 school year. As they remain committed to doing what is best for students, and listening to the parents, educators, and students in the consortium, PARCC worked on a redesign of their test for the following years. They decreased testing time and the amount of tests students would need to take beginning in the 2015-2016 school year.

How Can the Lumos Study Program Prepare Students for PARCC Tests?

At Lumos Learning, we believe that year-long learning and adequate practice before the actual test are the keys to success on these standardized tests. We have designed the Lumos study program to help students get plenty of realistic practice before the test and to promote year-long collaborative learning.

This is a Lumos **tedBook™**. It connects you to Online Workbooks and additional resources using  a number of devices including Android phones, iPhones, tablets and personal computers. The Lumos StepUp Online Workbooks are designed to promote year-long learning. It is a simple program students can securely access using a computer or device with internet access. It consists of hundreds of grade appropriate questions, aligned to the new Common Core State Standards. Students will get instant feedback and can review their answers anytime. Each student's answers and progress can be reviewed by parents and educators to reinforce the learning experience.

How to use this book effectively

The Lumos Program is a flexible learning tool. It can be adapted to suit a student's skill level and the time available to practice before standardized tests. Here are some tips to help you use this book and the online workbooks effectively:

Students

- Take one Summative Assessment (SA).
- Use the "Related Lumos StepUp® Online Workbook" in the Answer Key section to identify the topic that is related to each question.
- Use the Online workbooks to practice your areas of difficulty and complement classroom learning.
- Download the Lumos StepUp® app using the instructions provided in "How can I Download the App" to have anywhere access to online resources.
- Have open-ended questions evaluated by a teacher or parent, keeping in mind the scoring rubrics.
- Review additional questions in the practice area of the book.
- Take the second Summative Assessment as you get close to the test date.
- Complete the test in a quiet place, following the test guidelines. Practice tests provide you an opportunity to improve your test taking skills and to review topics included in the PARCC test.

Parents

- Familiarize yourself with the PARCC test format and expectations.
- Get useful information about your school by downloading the Lumos SchoolUp™ app. Please follow directions provided in "How to download Lumos SchoolUp™ App" section of this chapter.
- Help your child use Lumos StepUp® Online Workbooks by following the instructions in "How to access the Lumos Online Workbooks" section of this chapter.
- Help your child download the Lumos StepUp® app using the instructions provided in "How can I Download the App" section of this chapter.
- Review your child's performance in the "Lumos Online Workbooks" periodically. You can do this by simply asking your child to log into the system online and selecting the subject area you wish to review.
- Review your child's work in the practice Summative Assessments and Practice Section.

Teachers

- You can use the Lumos online programs along with this book to complement and extend your classroom instruction.

- Get a Free Teacher account by visiting LumosLearning.com/a/stepupbasic

  This Lumos StepUp® Basic account will help you:

  - Create up to 30 student accounts.
  - Review the online work of your students.
  - Easily access CCSS.
  - Create and share information about your classroom or school events.
  - Get insights into students' strengths and weakness in specific content areas.

  NOTE: There is a limit of one grade and subject per teacher for the free account.

- Download the Lumos SchoolUp™ mobile app using the instructions provided in "How can I download the App" section of this chapter.

PARCC Frequently Asked Questions

What Will PARCC English Language Assessments Look Like?

In many ways, the PARCC assessments will be unlike anything many students have ever seen. The tests will be conducted online, requiring students complete tasks to assess a deeper understanding of the CCSS. The students will be assessed once 75% of the year has been completed in one Summative based assessment and the Summative Assessment will be broken into three units: Unit 1, Unit 2, and Unit 3.

The test will consist of a combination of three new types of questions:

EBSR (Evidence Based Selected Response) – students will need to use evidence to prove their answer, choices will be often be given.

TECR (Technology Enhanced Constructed Response) – students will use technology to show comprehension. For example, they may be asked to drag and drop, cut and paste, or highlight their responses.

PCRs (Prose Constructed Response(s)) – students will be required to construct written response to a test prompt using specific evidence and details from the passages they have read.

The time for each ELA unit is described below:

Estimated Time on Task in Minutes			
Grade	Unit 1	Unit 2	Unit 3
3	90	75	90
4	90	90	90
5	90	90	90
6	110	110	90
7	110	110	90
8	110	110	90

What is a PARCC Aligned Test Practice Book?

Inside this book, you will find two full-length practice tests that are similar to the PARCC tests students will take to assess their mastery of CCSS aligned curriculum. Completing these tests will help students master the different areas that are included in newly aligned standardized tests and practice test taking skills. The results will help the students and educators get insights into students' strengths and weaknesses in specific content areas. These insights could be used to help students strengthen their skills in difficult topics and to improve speed and accuracy while taking the test.

LumosLearning.com

In addition, this book also contains a Practice Section with passages and questions broken into the key categories students will see in the three Summative Units: Literary text, Research Simulation (Informational text), and Narrative Writing.

How is this Lumos tedBook aligned to PARCC Guidelines?

Although the PARCC assessments will be conducted online, the practice tests here have been created to accurately reflect the depth and rigor of PARCC tasks in a pencil and paper format. Students will still be exposed to the TECR technology style questions so they become familiar with the wording and how to think through these types of tasks.

How to access the Lumos Online Workbooks

First Time Access:

Using a personal computer with internet access:	Using a smart phone or tablet:
Go to **http://www.lumoslearning.com/book** Enter the following access code in the Access Code field and press the Submit button. Access Code: PG3L-326-59-P 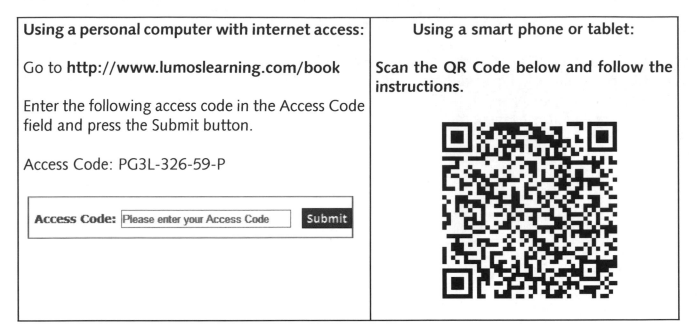	Scan the **QR Code** below and follow the instructions.

In the next screen, click on the "New User" button to register your user name and password.

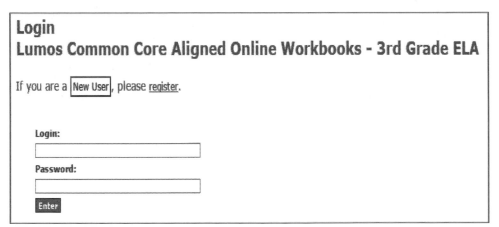

Subsequent Access:

After you establish your user id and password for subsequent access, simply login with your account information.

What if I buy more than one Lumos Study Program?

Please note that you can use all Online Workbooks with one User ID and Password. If you buy more than one book, you will access them with the same account.

Go back to the **http://www.lumoslearning.com/book** link and enter the access code provided in the second book. In the next screen simply login using your previously created account.

LumosLearning.com

Lumos StepUp® Mobile App
FAQ For Students

What is the Lumos StepUp® App?

It is a FREE application you can download onto your Android smart phones, tablets, iPhones, and iPads.

What are the Benefits of the StepUp® App?

This mobile application gives convenient access to Practice Tests, Common Core State Standards, Online Workbooks, and learning resources through your smart phone and tablet computers.

- Eleven Technology enhanced question types in both MATH and ELA
- Sample questions for Arithmetic drills
- Standard specific sample questions
- Instant access to the Common Core State Standards
- Jokes and cartoons to make learning fun!

Do I Need the StepUp® App to Access Online Workbooks?

No, you can access Lumos StepUp® Online Workbooks through a personal computer. The StepUp® app simply enhances your learning experience and allows you to conveniently access StepUp® Online Workbooks and additional resources through your smart phone or tablet.

How can I Download the App?

Visit **lumoslearning.com/a/stepup-app** using your smart phone or tablet and follow the instructions to download the app.

**QR Code
for Smart Phone
Or Tablet Users**

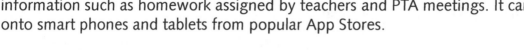

Lumos SchoolUp™ Mobile App FAQ
For Parents and Teachers

What is the Lumos SchoolUp™ App?

It is a free app that teachers can use to easily access real-time student activity information as well as assign learning resources to students. Parents can also use it to easily access school-related information such as homework assigned by teachers and PTA meetings. It can be downloaded onto smart phones and tablets from popular App Stores.

What are the Benefits of the Lumos SchoolUp™ App?

It provides convenient access to
- Real-time student activity information.
- School "Stickies". A Sticky could be information about an upcoming test, homework, extra curricular activities and other school events. Parents and educators can easily create their own sticky and share with the school community.
- Discover useful educational videos and mobile apps.
- Common Core State Standards.
- Educational blogs.
- StepUp™ student activity reports.

How can I Download the App?

Visit **lumoslearning.com/a/schoolup-app** using your smartphone or tablet and follow the instructions provided to download the App. Alternatively, scan the QR Code provided below using your smartphone or tablet computer.

QR Code
for Smart Phone
Or Tablet Users

         LumosLearning.com

Test Taking Tips

1) **The day before the test, make sure you get a good night's sleep.**

2) **On the day of the test, be sure to eat a good hearty breakfast! Also, be sure to arrive at school on time.**

3) **During the test:**

- **Read every question carefully.**

  - Do not spend too much time on any one question. Work steadily through all questions in the section.
  - Attempt all of the questions even if you are not sure of some answers.
  - If you run into a difficult question, eliminate as many choices as you can and then pick the best one from the remaining choices. Intelligent guessing will help you increase your score.
  - Also, mark the question so that if you have extra time, you can return to it after you reach the end of the section. Try to erase the marks after you complete the work.
  - Some questions may refer to a graph, chart, or other kind of picture. Carefully review the graphic before answering the question.
  - Be sure to include explanations for your written responses and show all work.

- **While Answering Multiple-Choice (EBSR) questions.**

  - Completely fill in the bubble corresponding to your answer choice.
  - Read all of the answer choices, even if think you have found the correct answer.

- **While Answering TECR questions.**

  - Read the directions of each question. Some might ask you to drag something, others to select, and still others to highlight. Follow all instructions of the question (or questions if it is in multiple parts)

Prose Constructed Response (PCR) Rubric

Each Summative Assessment includes different writing tasks which will be scored by hand. In order to effectively assess students' writing, a standardized rubric will be use. The following rubric will be used throughout this workbook as a means of assessing the writing prompts. Students should be familiar with the rubric as it is an excellent guide to the type of responses they should be creating. The Detailed Answer section of each Summative Assessment will include the page number of the rubric so students can see the scoring guide.

Literary & Informational Rubric

4 Point Score	3 Point Score	2 Point Score	1 Point Score	0 Point Score
The student response fully and thoughtfully addresses all parts of the prompt.	The student response addresses all parts of the prompt.	The student response addresses basic parts of the prompt.	The student response addresses limited parts of the prompt.	The student response addresses no parts of the prompt.
The student response demonstrates a full and thorough understanding of what it is written explicitly in the text.	The student response demonstrates an effective understanding of what it is written explicitly in the text.	The student response demonstrates some understanding of what it is written explicitly in the text.	The student response demonstrates a minimal understanding of most of the concepts written explicitly in the text.	The student response demonstrates little or no understanding of most of the concepts written explicitly in the text.
The student response demonstrates a full and thorough analysis of the text by making accurate and meaningful inferences from the text.	The student response demonstrates a mostly thorough analysis of the text by making accurate and meaningful inferences from the text.	The student response demonstrates some analysis of the text by making accurate reasonable inferences from the text.	The student response demonstrates an attempt at analysis of the text by making inferences that are supported, in part, by the text.	The student response makes little or no attempt at analysis of the text by making inferences, or inferences or not reasonable and not supported by the text.
The student response is completely and intentionally supported by explicit references from the text.	The student response is completely and intentionally supported by explicit references from the text.	The student response is somewhat supported by intentional, explicit references from the text.	The student response is supported by limited, general or vague references from the text.	The student response is supported is not intentionally supported by references from the text.
The student response is effectively organized, clear, and has an effective style.	The student response is mostly organized, clear, and has a mostly effective style.	The student response has some organization and is somewhat clear with a somewhat effective style.	The student response has limited organization and clarity and is written in a minimally effective style.	The student response has no organization, is not clear, and/or has no, or an inappropriate, style.

Narrative Rubric

4 Point Score	3 Point Score	2 Point Score	1 Point Score	0 Point Score
The student response is developed effectively, has narrative elements, and remains consistent to the task.	The student response is developed mostly effectively, has most narrative elements, and remains mostly consistent to the task.	The student response is developed somewhat effective, has general narrative elements, and remains somewhat consistent to the task.	The student response is developed minimally, has limited narrative elements and limited consistency to the task.	The student response is not developed and is inappropriate to the task.
The student response is effectively organized, clear, and has an effective style.	The student response is mostly organized, clear, and has a mostly effective style.	The student response has some organization and is somewhat clear with a somewhat effective style.	The student response has limited organization and clarity and is written in a minimally effective style.	The student response has no organization, is not clear, and/or has no, or an inappropriate, style.
The student response shows full understanding and application of conventions of the English. There may be some minor errors in grammar, mechanics, and word usage. The mean is effective and clear.	The student response shows full understanding and application of the conventions of English. There may be a few minor errors in grammar, mechanics, and word usage. The mean is effective and clear.	The student response shows some understanding and application of the conventions of English. There may be minor errors in grammar, mechanics, and word usage. The meaning is somewhat effective and generally clear.	The student response shows limited understanding and application of the conventions of English. There may be some minor errors in grammar, mechanics, and word usage. The mean is generally clear.	The student response shows no real understanding and application of the conventions of English. There may be frequent and varied errors in grammar, mechanics, and word usage. The mean is ineffective and unclear.

Summative Assessment (SA) - 1

Student Name:

Test Date:

Start Time:

End Time:

> **Here are some reminders for when you are taking the Grade 3 ELA Summative Assessment (SA)**
>
> To answer the questions on the test, use the directions given in the question. If you do not know the answer to a question, skip it and go on to the next question. If time permits, you may return to questions in this session only. Do your best to answer every question.

Unit 1

Read "The Secret" and answer the questions that follow.

The Secret
by Carla Gajewskey

1. One morning Janie Rose woke up to a big crash in her room. She opened her eyes slowly, scared of what she might find.

2. She saw her unpacked boxes from the move scattered on the floor. Janie screamed in her pillow, "I wish I never had to move!"

3. Janie's mom got a new job which moved Janie from her school, soccer team, and friends.

4. Janie got out of bed and went downstairs to fix a bowl of cereal for breakfast. Her mom was already down there and told Janie good morning. Janie mumbled something that sounded like a good morning.

5. Her mom sat down beside Janie and tried to make her feel better by telling her that she would meet new friends and to give this town a chance. Janie just rolled her eyes, and slurped the milk up from her cereal bowl.

6. Janie then got up and went back to her room. She crawled back in bed and pulled her covers up to her chin. She stared at the window, and the old chest underneath it. The chest was there when they moved in.

         LumosLearning.com   ▲

7. Janie got out of bed and walked over to see what was in it. She opened it up to find many neat treasures. She found dolls, hair bows, colors, and a rolled up piece of paper.

8. She opened up the paper to find that it was a map. The map title read, *The Secret of Blue Ridge.* "Hmmm, that is the name of this town," Janie said.

9. As Janie studied the map she realized that this big secret was at Blue Ridge Library. Janie got herself ready and ran down the stairs with the map.

10. She grabbed an apple and told her mom she was headed to the library as she was running out the door. Janie's mom yelled, "You don't even know where the library is!"

Janie yelled, "I have a map!"

11. Janie hopped on her bike and looked at the compass rose. The compass rose showed that the library was north of her house.

12. Janie then compared the map symbols to the map key. The map symbols showed Janie that she would pass Bert's Grocery, Amelia's Flowers, and Carl's Cars.

13. As Janie followed the map she saw a soccer field with a group of girls playing on it. She stopped for a moment and just watched them.

14. One of the girls ran up to Janie and asked her if she wanted to play. Janie gave a slight smile and said, "Maybe, but I have to take care of something first."

15. She rode all the way to the library and parked her bike. She went into the library and read the clue on the back of the map.

16. The clue read, *look to the stars.* "Look to the stars," Janie said while looking up.

17. Then Janie saw a quote etched on the ceiling. "Make today, better than yesterday, and tomorrow better than today." Janie thought for a moment and realized that is the secret.

18. She smiled and said, "Now I think I have a soccer game to play."

1.   **Part A**

What is the meaning of the word <u>scattered</u> as it is used in paragraphs 1 and 2?

Ⓐ **Neat**
Ⓑ **Unpacked**
Ⓒ **Thrown about**
Ⓓ **Leaking**

Part B

Which detail from the story best supports the answer to Part A?

Ⓐ One morning Janie Rose woke up to a big crash in her room. She opened her eyes slowly scared of what she might find.
Ⓑ Janie screamed in her pillow, "I wish I never had to move!"
Ⓒ She crawled back in bed and pulled her covers up to her chin.
Ⓓ Janie got out of bed and walked over to see what was in it.

2. In the box below, write the letter of the phrase from the paragraph that helps the reader know that Janie did not want to move.

Ⓐ She smiled and said, "Now I think I have a soccer game to play."
Ⓑ Then Janie saw a quote etched on the ceiling. "Make today, better than yesterday, and tomorrow better than today."
Ⓒ Janie got out of bed and walked over to see what was in it.
Ⓓ Her mom sat down beside Janie and tried to make her feel better by telling her that she will meet new friends and to give this town a chance.

```
give this town a chance
```

3. What is the meaning of the secret of Blue Ridge that she found?

Ⓐ See the bright side of things.
Ⓑ Live life to the fullest and always try to make your days good.
Ⓒ When you are making things good today, the future will automatically be good too.
Ⓓ Celebrate everything in your life, even the small things.

Read "Summer" and answer the questions that follow.

Summer
by Carla Gajewskey

1. What is summer?

2. Is it fresh cut green grass that tickles your toes?

3. Is it hours in the pool that wrinkles your hands?

4. Is it the sound of crickets that sing you a lullaby?

5. Could it be trips to the beach where the foamy sea grabs at your feet?

6. Maybe it is hiking trips where you reach the top of the tallest mountain and feel the wind play with your hair?

7. Is it the song from your little brother that cries, "Are we there yet," from the back seat on long road trips?

8. Is it the BOOM of fireworks on the fourth of July?

9. Could summer be picking blue berries or shelling peas?

10. Is summer, camping trips under the starry sky, or just a weekend at your grandma's house?

11. Is it running through the water sprinkler or jumping off of the diving board?

12. Is summer riding your bike all day, or just sleeping all day?

13. Well, yes, but summer is that and more.

14. It is cook outs, apple pies, lemonade, snow cones, roller coasters, camp outs, fishing, long days and the smell of sun screen all through the air.

15. Summer is a time where your imagination comes to life.

16. Summer is magical!

4.   **Part A**

What is the meaning of the word <u>wrinkles</u> as it is used in stanza 3 from the poem?

Ⓐ Pressed
Ⓑ Unsmoothed
Ⓒ Soft
Ⓓ Glossy

Part B

Which detail from the story best supports the answer to Part A?

Ⓐ Sound of crickets
Ⓑ Hours in the pool
Ⓒ The foamy sea that grabs your feet
Ⓓ The green cut grass that tickles your toes

5.   **Part A**

The author of this poem most likely does which of the following during the summer?

Ⓐ Go to work
Ⓑ Knit
Ⓒ Travel
Ⓓ Snow Ski

Part B

Which line from the poem supports the answer to part A?

Ⓐ Could it be trips to the beach where the foamy sea grabs at your feet?
Ⓑ Is it fresh cut green grass that tickles your toes?
Ⓒ Is it the BOOM of fireworks on the fourth of July?
Ⓓ Is summer riding your bike all day, or just sleeping all day?

6.   Select the most important description of summer as mentioned in the poem write it in the box below.

Ⓐ Sumer is the BOOM of fireworks on the fourth of July.
Ⓑ Summer is riding your bike all day.
Ⓒ Summer is a time where your imagination comes to life.
Ⓓ Sumer is the sound of crickets that sing you a lullaby.

```
┌─────────────────────────────────────────────────────┐
│                                                       │
│                                                       │
│                                                       │
│                                                       │
└─────────────────────────────────────────────────────┘
```

7.   You have read a story "The Secret" and a poem "Summer." Write an Essay describing Janie from "The Secret." For the character, Janie, describe:

• Explain how the thoughts, words, and or actions of the character help you understand what the character is like.
• Explain what Janie's summer would look like in her new town if she became friends with the author of the poem "Summer."
• Be sure to use evidence from the passages

```
┌─────────────────────────────────────────────────────┐
│                                                       │
├─────────────────────────────────────────────────────┤
│                                                       │
├─────────────────────────────────────────────────────┤
│                                                       │
├─────────────────────────────────────────────────────┤
│                                                       │
├─────────────────────────────────────────────────────┤
│                                                       │
├─────────────────────────────────────────────────────┤
│                                                       │
├─────────────────────────────────────────────────────┤
│                                                       │
├─────────────────────────────────────────────────────┤
│                                                       │
└─────────────────────────────────────────────────────┘
```

LumosLearning.com

Read "The Race" and answer the questions that follow.

The Race
by Carla Gajewskey

1. Jack was the fastest rabbit in California.

2. Jack also thought he was the most handsome rabbit in California. He was skinny like a green bean. His ears stood straight up on his head, and they were as tall as the Empire State Building. Jack's fur was gray and fluffy.

3. Jack did not just hop about through the brush, but his skinny body almost flew through the brush. He hopped so fast that you never even saw his feet hit the ground.

4. One day he saw a flyer inviting all rabbits to enter the 35th annual Rabbit Run. The winner would win the gold trophy cup filled with the juiciest carrots from Farmer Brown's garden.

5. Jack knew he had to sign up. After he signed up he began to practice. Jack had one week before the race and he wanted to be ready.

6. On the day of the race Jack saw rabbits from all over. He saw tiny rabbits, medium size rabbits, large rabbits, short eared rabbits, and long eared rabbits, white rabbits, black rabbits, spotted rabbits, and all different kinds of rabbits.

7. One of the rabbits had long ears that hung to the floor. He hopped up to Jack and said, "Hi, my name is Marty. I'm from Jackson County. I'm going to win that carrot cup for my Mamma. She has 7 baby rabbits that need tending to. What is your name?"

Jack just said, "Jack."

8. Marty continued to talk and talk like Jack was his best friend. Marty talked about his brothers and sisters, Farmer Brown, how barley is good for you, and so much more.

9. Jack listened and looked disturbed.

10. Once it was time for the race, all of the rabbits lined up. Marty lined up by Jack and wished him luck.

11. Once the race started Jack was off and all you could see was a cloud of dust. As Jack was looking behind himself he ran right into a thorn bush and got tangled up.

12. The other rabbits began to pass him by, yet no one stopped to help except Marty. Jack said, "Marty what are you doing? You need to go so you can win the cup of carrots for you mamma."

Marty said, "You should always stop and help someone in need and everything else will work out."

13. Jack felt very bad for feeling annoyed with Marty earlier.

14. Once he got out of the thorn bush, Marty asked Jack if he wanted to race and gave him a wink.

15. Jack said okay and shook his head and smiled. They asked Lawrence a lizard to tell them when to go. Lawrence said, "On your Mark. Get Set. Go!"

16. Jack started hopping into a cloud of dust. Marty just left him in the dust. Marty caught up to everybody and left them in the dust. Marty hopped through the finish line to the gold cup of carrots.

17. Jack shook Marty's paw and laughing asked him how he did it. Marty said, "It is just the way I am made. My ears hang down so when I run they do not catch the wind like yours. I do not have anything to hold me back."

18. Jack congratulated Marty and started to walk off. Marty yelled, "Come have some juicy carrots with me." Jack said, "I thought they were for your family?"

Marty said, "They are! Friends are family too!"

LumosLearning.com

8. **Part A**

At the beginning of the story Jack only cares about himself. What happens in the following paragraphs that start to change Jack?

Ⓐ Jack won the race.
Ⓑ Marty helps Jack.
Ⓒ Marty won the race.
Ⓓ Lawrence and Jack became friends.

Part B

Which paragraph supports the answer to Part A?

Ⓐ Paragraph 11
Ⓑ Paragraph 15
Ⓒ Paragraph 16
Ⓓ Paragraph 12

9. In the box below write the correct answer for the feeling that Jack had about Marty at the end of the story?

Ⓐ Mad
Ⓑ Annoyed
Ⓒ Friendly
Ⓓ Disappointed

Feeling | Friendly |

10. In the box below, write the letter of the phrase from the paragraph that helps the reader understand that one of the morals of "The Race" is friendships form when you least expect it.

Ⓐ The other rabbits began to pass him by, yet no one stopped to help except Marty.
Ⓑ Jack just listened and looked disturbed.
Ⓒ Marty lined up by Jack and wished him luck.
Ⓓ He hopped up to Jack and said, "Hi, my name is Marty. I'm from Jackson County."

| A |

11. (Part A)

Jack was described as being, "skinny like a green bean." What does Jack look like?

Ⓐ Green
Ⓑ Fat
Ⓒ Thin
Ⓓ Smelly

Part B

What detail from the story supports the answer to Part A?

Ⓐ Jack did not just hop about through the brush, but his skinny body almost flew through the brush.
Ⓑ His ears stood straight up on his head, and they were as tall as the Empire State Building.
Ⓒ He saw tiny rabbits, medium size rabbits, large rabbits, short eared rabbits, and long eared rabbits, white rabbits, black rabbits, spotted rabbits, and all different kinds of rabbits.
Ⓓ Jack also thought he was the most handsome rabbit in California.

12. What type of figurative language is the description of Jack's ears in paragraph 2?

Ⓐ Similie   what do they mean?
Ⓑ Metaphor
Ⓒ Hyperbole
Ⓓ Alliteration

Unit 2

Read "Is the Moon Really Made of Cheese?" and answer the questions that follow.

Is the Moon Really Made of Cheese?
by Carla Gajewskey

1. What a tasty treat it would be if the moon was made of cheese. Sadly, the moon is not made from cheese but from rocks.

2. Scientists believe that 4.5 billion years ago a large object hit the Earth. Rocks flew out everywhere from this and orbited the Earth. The rocks melted together and then cooled down. For billions of years after that, rocks kept hitting the Moon. This caused big pits on the surface of the Moon. From Earth these big holes look like a face. This is where the saying, "The man on the moon," comes from.

3. The Earth has an atmosphere. This Atmosphere is a layer of gas that surrounds a planet. This is why we have oxygen to breathe. The moon does not have an atmosphere. This is why astronauts have to wear space suits and helmets. It protects them and provides oxygen that the moon does not have.

4. You may wonder why the moon is bright like a star if it is just made of rock. The moon looks bright because the sun light reflects off of the moon. This makes it look like the moon is lit up. As the moon goes around the Earth we see the sunlit part of the moon. That is why you see the moon go from a banana shape, also known as a crescent, to a full moon and back to a crescent in a month's time. These shapes are called the phases of the moon. The moon is more than a pretty lit up rock in the sky. The gravity of the moon pulls at the Earth. This pull causes two high tides on the Earth every day.

5. The Moon has been of interest to people since the beginning of their being. It wasn't till the 1600s that a man by the name of Galileo made maps of the moon. Galileo never walked on the moon, but used a telescope. He developed a telescope that could make objects look bigger up to 20 times. He was able to see the surface of the moon. This was only the beginning.

6. As time went on, those maps would be used to explore the moon. The first person to walk on the moon was Neil Armstrong. On July 21, 1969 his space craft, the Eagle, landed on the moon. He then did what many people only dream of doing. He set foot on the moon. He wore a huge space suit and space mask. He had to wear this because the moon was airless, waterless, and lifeless. He then said these famous words, "That is one small step for man, one giant leap for mankind." These words are used to this day. They are a reminder of how far we have come, and how far we will go.

13. **Part A**

What is the meaning of the word <u>pit</u> as the narrator uses it in paragraph 2 of, *Is the Moon Really Made of Cheese?*

Ⓐ Stars
Ⓑ Holes
Ⓒ Dents
Ⓓ Hills

Part B

Which detail from the story best supports the answer to Part A?

Ⓐ The gravity of the moon pulls at the Earth.
Ⓑ Sadly, the moon is not made from cheese but from rocks.
Ⓒ From Earth these big holes look like a face.
Ⓓ You may wonder why the moon is bright like a star if it is just made of rock.

14. **Part A**

What is the purpose of the telescope?

Ⓐ to make faraway objects look smaller
Ⓑ to make faraway objects look bigger
Ⓒ to make faraway objects look the same
Ⓓ to help people who wear glasses see better

Part B

Choose one detail from the article that supports the answer to part A. Write the number of the paragraph in the box below.

Supporting Detail ☐

15. Why is the phrase Neil Armstrong said when he landed on the moon such an important saying?

Ⓐ He went where many people dream of going.
Ⓑ Because of the weightlessness, each small step became a giant leap.
Ⓒ Although he only took a small step, that one step was important for all men.
Ⓓ His space suit was so big that even his small step seemed huge.

Read "Maps" and answer the questions that follow.

Maps
by Carla Gajewskey

1. Have you ever heard the story of Hansel and Gretel? Two children are left in the woods by their mean step-mother. She takes them far into the woods so they cannot find their way back home.

2. Hansel and Gretel tear off pieces of bread and throw it behind them. They did this so they could follow the bread crumbs back home.

3. There is one big problem already, and we haven't even got to the evil witch yet. Animals live in the woods, and love to eat bread. A bird finds their breadcrumbs and eats them. When Hansel and Gretel are ready to go home their trail is gone. If they would have used real landmarks, they would be able to find their way home.

4. It is a good thing we have maps. A map is a picture that shows you where things are. Pirates used maps to find treasure. Explorers made maps as they discovered new lands. Your sister may have made a map that leads to her diary.

5. Maps can be as big as the world or as small as a city. Every map is made up of a map title, map symbol, map key, distance scale, compass rose, and cardinal directions. These are the things that help you read the map.

6. The map title tells you what the map is about. If it is about your town then the title will be your town's name. The map symbols are pictures that mean different things. The map key tells you what those things are. So if there is a symbol of a cross on your map the map key might say it is a church. Also, a picture of an airplane shows an airport.

7. The distance scale is used to help you measure how far it is between two places. The compass rose is a drawing that is made up of the four cardinal directions, north, south, east, and west.

8. Some maps are found on paper. Paper maps are being used less and less. The reason for this is many maps today are electronic.

9. The ones that are found on smartphones and GPS systems use a satellite to give the most up to date directions. Some of them even give you verbal directions with the map.

10. A map is a useful tool whether it is written or electronic. Just think how the story of Hansel and Gretel would have ended if they knew how to make a map of where they were going or where they had been.

16. **Part A**

   What is the meaning of the word landmark as it is used in paragraph 3?

   Ⓐ GPS
   Ⓑ Map
   Ⓒ Compass
   Ⓓ A well-known object on a piece of land

   Part B

   What word from the story best supports the answer to Part A?

   Ⓐ Real
   Ⓑ Maps
   Ⓒ Breadcrumbs
   Ⓓ Compass

17. **Part A**

   Where would a picture of a landmark be found on a map?

   Ⓐ Map Title
   Ⓑ Compass Rose
   Ⓒ Map Key
   Ⓓ Distance scale

   Part B

   Which detail from the story provides the best evidence for the answer to Part A?

   Ⓐ The distance scale is used to help you measure how far it is between two places.
   Ⓑ The map key tells you what things are on a map.
   Ⓒ The compass rose is a drawing that is made up of the four cardinal directions: north, south, east, and west.
   Ⓓ The map title tells you what the map is about.

LumosLearning.com ▲

18. **Read the list of possible supporting details below. Select three details that support the main idea as it is listed.**

Possible Supporting Details

Ⓐ A map is a picture that shows you where things are.
Ⓑ Pirates used maps to find treasure.
Ⓒ Maps can be as big as the world or as small as a city.
Ⓓ Every map is made up of a map title, map symbol, map key, distance scale, compass rose, and cardinal directions.
Ⓔ Explorers made maps as they discovered new lands.
Ⓕ These are the things that help you read the map.
Ⓖ Your sister may have made a map that leads to her diary.

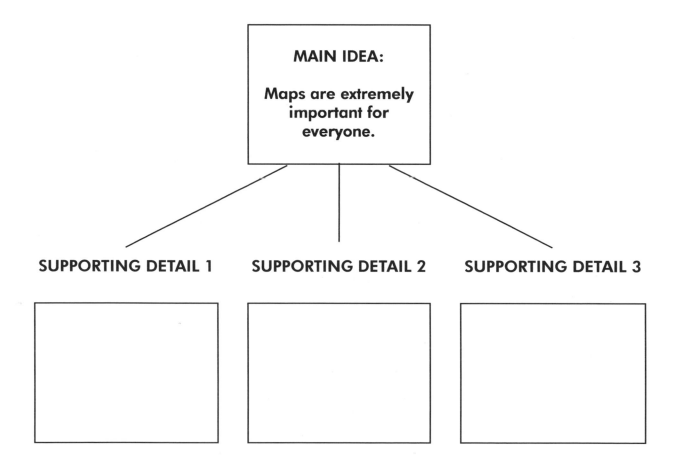

MAIN IDEA:

Maps are extremely important for everyone.

SUPPORTING DETAIL 1   SUPPORTING DETAIL 2   SUPPORTING DETAIL 3

19. Using the informational story "Maps," and the information of what the moon looks like from "Is the Moon Really Made of Cheese" write an essay on what your map of the moon would look like if you were Galileo.

Please include the Map title of your map, Map Symbols, and Map Key.

 LumosLearning.com

Unit 3

Read the poem "Home" and answer the questions that follow.

Home
by Carla Gajewskey

1.   There is a big oak tree in the middle of Central Park.
      It is the home of the beautiful ebony chested, horned lark.
      Why did he come there from his home in the tundra?
      Maybe to see his friend Cassandra.

2.   She is a sparrow that sits with him on the very top limb.
      They sing together until the sun sinks low and the day becomes dim.
      They sleep on their limb found on the big oak tree in the middle of Central Park.
      They find a cluster of leaves to shelter them from the rain when the sky turns dark.

3.   There is a hole in the trunk, made from a woodpecker, that they use when it is cold.
      The birds stay in there till the weather turns warm and the sun shines like gold.
      They find their dinner in the bark and leaves.
      The bugs and seeds there is what they seize.

4.   They fly over the park to stretch their wings,
      And watch the small children fly like birds on the swings.
      There is a big oak tree in the middle of central park.
      It is the home of the beautiful ebony chested, horned lark.

5.   Why did he come there
      from his home in the tundra?
      Because the big oak tree, in the middle of Central Park
      is the home of Cassandra and the lark.

20.   **Part A**

What is the meaning of the word <u>cluster</u> as it is used in stanza 2?

Ⓐ One
Ⓑ Group
Ⓒ Tiny
Ⓓ Green

Part B

Which detail from the story best supports the answer to part A?

Ⓐ Leaves to shelter them from the rain when the sky turns dark.
Ⓑ They sleep on their limb found on the big oak tree in the middle of Central Park.
Ⓒ She is a sparrow that sits with him on the very top limb.
Ⓓ There is a hole in the trunk.

21.   In the box below, write the letters of the three details of the story to create the setting.

Ⓐ There is a big oak tree in the middle of Central Park.
Ⓑ It is the home of the beautiful ebony chested, horned lark.
Ⓒ Maybe to see his friend Cassandra.
Ⓓ There is a hole in the trunk, made from a woodpecker, that they use when it turns cold.
Ⓔ They sleep on their limb found on the big oak tree in the middle of central park.
Ⓕ Why did he come there from his home in the tundra?

Setting ⌷⌷⌷⌷⌷⌷⌷⌷⌷⌷⌷⌷⌷⌷⌷⌷⌷⌷⌷⌷⌷⌷

22.   Which statement best expresses one of the themes of the poem?

Ⓐ Moving can be hard.
Ⓑ It is important to visit friends.
Ⓒ Singing makes you feel better.
Ⓓ Home is where friends and family are.

23.   **Which detail from the story provides the best evidence for the answer to Part A?**

Ⓐ It is the home of the beautiful ebony chested, horned lark.
Ⓑ Why did he come there from his home in the tundra?
Ⓒ Because the big oak tree, in the middle of Central Park is the home of Cassandra and the lark.
Ⓓ They sing together until the sun sinks low and the day becomes dim.

24.   **Which phrases best describe the lark?**

Ⓐ ebony chested and horned
Ⓑ big oak tree, in the middle of Central Park
Ⓒ cluster of leaves to shelter
Ⓓ weather turns warm and the sun shines like gold

25.   **Think of a friend you have, in or out of school. Tell one story that comes to mind when you think of this friend.**

LumosLearning.com

Read "Henry Ford" and "Boom, Crash, Bang" and answer the questions that follow.

Henry Ford
by Carla Gajewskey

1. Henry Ford was born on a farm in Michigan. He did not like farm work. Henry Ford dreamed of moving to the city. Even at an early age he was good at building things. He knew he would someday find a job.

2. At age 16, he moved to the city of Detroit, Michigan. He found a job as a machinist. A machinist uses tools and machines to make parts out of metal or wood. This was hard and dangerous work. Many workers got hurt while making parts.

3. Henry Ford tinkered with the gasoline engine. He worked on motors for fun. He used his money for his hobby. Henry Ford put a motor on what looked like a wagon. Later, he worked with Thomas Edison, the inventor of the light bulb. Thomas Edison liked Henry Ford's idea. In 1898, Henry Ford made his second gas car.

4. Henry Ford started out with groups of two or three workers to put the cars together. He knew he needed the best workers he could find. He paid five dollars a day for the best help. His team used parts from other businesses. This made the cars cost a lot of money.

5. He is most famous for the assembly line. Henry Ford made the assembly line better so he could make more cars. In an assembly line, each worker has a job. The car moves in a line to be put together.

6. It was all downhill after that. Ford's company grew rapidly. Soon his company was not just in Michigan but all over the world.

7. Today, people drive cars made by the Ford Motor Company. The Beach Boys wrote a song about a Ford car. The song was called, "Fun, Fun, and Fun 57 T-Bird." Henry Ford's cars also made it in the movies. The 1967 Ford Mustang was in the movie, *Gone in 60 Seconds*. Henry Ford's cars are loved by many. Henry Ford died on April 7, 1947. His dream did not die with him but lives on through Ford Motor Company.

Boom, Crash, Bang

1. Boom, crash, bang! That was the sound right before it happened.

2. It started out as a normal morning. I climbed into my baby blue car. I cranked it up and listened to the engine purr as it warmed up. I ran my fingers over the silver, galloping mustang on the center of my steering wheel. Then, I turned on my radio to my favorite radio station. The smell of leather filled my nose as I got comfortable in my seat.

3. Once I was ready, I backed out of my driveway and took off. The pipes roared as I went faster and faster down the open road.

4. The sun painted the black sky with red and orange colors. The birds were perched on the power lines, singing a good morning song as I drove past them. I could not have asked for a better morning.

5. Then, it happened. I stopped at the red light right in front of my work. As I waited for the light to turn green I saw a truck in my rear view mirror coming closer and closer. Before I knew it, his car hit the back of mine. Boom, crash, bang! As it happened, I braced myself.

6. Once the damage was done I looked around me and realized that I was okay. Then that sinking feeling hit the pit of my stomach. I yelled, "My car! My beautiful, baby blue car!"

7. I got out of my car and raced to the back of it. I saw the man already standing outside in front of his looking at the damage. I closed my eyes and barely opened one at a time. The whole rear end of my car was dented in. This would have made Henry Ford himself want to cry.

8. The man apologized and we were both relieved that neither one of us were hurt. We exchanged insurance information and waited for the police to arrive.

9. I started looking for the best body shop for my baby blue car. She only deserved the best since she is the prettiest 1967 Mustang Ford ever made.

From the story "Henry Ford"

26.   **Part A**

Henry Ford's company started out with a group of workers producing only a few cars in a small factory in Michigan. Through time and hard work his company grew worldwide. What major change did Henry Ford make to help his company grow to this level?

Ⓐ Henry Ford created an assembly line
Ⓑ Henry Ford went back to farming
Ⓒ Henry Ford worked with Thomas Edison
Ⓓ Henry Ford made the Ford Mustang

Part B

Which detail from the story best supports the answer to Part A?

Ⓐ Later, he worked with Thomas Edison, the inventor of the light bulb.
Ⓑ It was all downhill after that. Ford's company grew rapidly. Soon his company was not just in Michigan but all over the world.
Ⓒ Henry Ford made the assembly line better so he could make more cars.
Ⓓ Henry Ford started out with groups of two or three workers to put the cars together.

From the Story "Crash, Boom, Bang"

27.   **Part A**

The main idea of "Crash, Boom, Bang" is

Ⓐ The narrator got into a fender bender
Ⓑ The narrator was driving to work
Ⓒ The narrator loves her car
Ⓓ The narrator wanted a new car

Part B

Write the letter of the detail that supports the answer to Part A.

Ⓐ I cranked it up and listened to the engine purr as it warmed up.
Ⓑ Then I turned on my radio to my favorite radio station.
Ⓒ She only deserved the best since she is the prettiest 1967 Mustang Ford every made.
Ⓓ Before I knew it his car hit the back of mine. Boom, crash, bang!

From the stories "Henry Ford" and "Boom, Crash, Bang"

28. When the car in "Boom, Crash, Bang" was hit, the narrator said it would have made Henry Ford want to cry. Why would that accident make Henry Ford want to cry?

    Ⓐ Henry Ford was the narrator's dad.
    Ⓑ The car that was hit was a Ford, and Henry Ford was the owner of Ford Motor Company.
    Ⓒ Henry Ford was in the car.
    Ⓓ The accident happened by Henry Ford's farm.

29. Choose one detail from the story "Henry Ford" and one detail from the story "Boom, Crash, Bang" that support the answer to Question 28. Write the number of the paragraph in the correct box below.

Supporting detail from "Henry Ford"

Supporting detail from "Boom, Crash, Bang"

30. Part A

What type of Ford car did the narrator drive in "Boom, Crash, Bang" that made it to the big movie screen as mentioned in "Henry Ford?"

    Ⓐ Ford F150
    Ⓑ Ford Thunderbird
    Ⓒ Ford Galaxy
    Ⓓ Ford Mustang

Part B

Choose the correct paragraph number from the story "Henry Ford" and the correct paragraph number from the story "Boom, Crash, Bang" that support the answer to Part A. Write the number of the paragraph in the correct box below.

Paragraph number from "Henry Ford"

Paragraph number from "Boom, Crash, Bang"

End of Summative Assessment (SA) - 1

     LumosLearning.com

Summative Assessment (SA) - 1

Answer Key

Question No.	Answer	Related Lumos Online Workbook	CCSS
		Unit 1	
1 PART A	C	Figurative Language Expressions	RL.3.4
1 PART B	A	Figurative Language Expressions	RL.3.4
2	D	The Question Session	RL.3.1
3	B	Tell Me Again...	RL.3.2
4 PART A	B	Figurative Language Expressions	RL.3.4
4 PART B	B	Figurative Language Expressions	RL.3.4
5 PART A	C	The Question Session	RL.3.1
5 PART B	A	Tell Me Again...; Caring Characters & Life's Lessons	RL.3.2
6	C	The Question Session	RL.3.1
7	*	Lets Talk!	W.3.3
8 PART A	B	Calling All Characters; A Chain of Events	RL.3.3
8 PART B	D	Calling All Characters; A Chain of Events	RL.3.3
9	C	Calling All Characters; A Chain of Events	RL.3.3
10	A	Tell Me Again...; Caring Characters & Life's Lessons	RL.3.2
11 PART A	C	Calling All Characters; A Chain of Events	RL 3.3
11 PART B	A	Calling All Characters; A Chain of Events	RL.3.3
12	C	Making Words Work	L.3.5
		Unit 2	
13 PART A	B	Educational Expressions	RI.3.4
13 PART B	C	Educational Expressions	RI.3.4
14 PART A	B		RI.3.1
14 PART B	Paragraph 5		RI.3.1
15	C	The Main Idea Arena	RI.3.2
16 PART A	D	Educational Expressions	RI.3.4
16 PART B	A	Educational Expressions	RI.3.4
17 PART A	C		RI.3.1
17 PART B	B		RI.3.1

* See detailed explanation

Question No.	Answer	Related Lumos Online Workbook	CCSS
18	B, E, and G	The Main Idea Arena	RI.3.2
19	*	Make Your Ideas Clearer; Connecting Ideas	W.3.2
Unit 3			
20 PART A	B	Figurative Language Expressions	RL.3.4
20 PART B	A	Figurative Language Expressions	RL.3.4
21	A, D, and E	Alike and Different	RL.3.9
22	D	Tell Me Again...; Caring Characters & Life's Lessons	RL.3.2
23	C	The Question Session	RL.3.1
24	A	The Question Session	RL.3.1
25	*	Lets Talk!	W.3.3
26 PART A	A		RI.3.1
26 PART B	C		RI.3.1
27 PART A	C	The Main Idea Arena	RI.3.2
27 PART B	C	The Main Idea Arena	RI.3.2
28	B		RI.3.9
29	7, 7 or 9		RI.3.9
30 PART A	D		RI.3.9
30 PART B	7, 9		RI.3.9

* See detailed explanation

Summative Assessment (SA) - 1

Detailed Explanations

Question No.	Answer	Detailed Explanation
		Unit 1
1 PART A	C	When things are scattered they are thrown about. A is incorrect because neat is the opposite of scattered. B is incorrect because although clues from the story did state that the boxes were unpacked, it was when they fell over that they became scattered. And D is incorrect because leaking normally applies to liquid.
1 PART B	A	When her boxes fell to the floor her items were thrown about. Option B explains how Janie was feeling when her box fell over and scattered it did not explain what scattered means. Option C was after she ate breakfast and her mom told her to "give this town a chance" –it had nothing to do with her scattered items. And Option D discusses when Janie was going to look in the chest
2	D	D is correct because Janie's mother was telling her to give this town a chance, and telling her she will meet new friends. A is incorrect because it tells how she finally accepts the town and plays a soccer game. B explains that she realized that she is going to make her life better and the move wasn't so bad. And C is incorrect because explains when Janie walks over to examine the chest
3	B	The secret saying, "make today better than yesterday and tomorrow better than today," reminds the reader to always live life to the fullest and look to make your days better.
4 PART A	B	Smoothed means to be without wrinkles or creases. When you add the word Un in front of smooth, it changes the meaning to not smooth, which means wrinkled.
4 PART B	B	Extended time in water causes the human skin to wrinkle. Therefore hours in the pool would cause wrinkles.
5 PART A	C	The summer activities the writer writes about lets the reader know that she has traveled some. The poem does not give any clues that the author goes to work, knits, or snow skis.
5 PART B	A	She spoke about trips to the beach. A trip could also mean travel. B, C, and D do not give examples of traveling anywhere. Those things could be done at home.

Question No.	Answer	Detailed Explanation
6	C	Although the poem lists many things that summer is, the fact that it's the time your imagination comes to life is the most important because then summer truly becomes magical.
7		See Rubric Page No. 10 & 11
8 PART A	B	At the beginning of the story details are given that help the reader infer that Jack is very self-centered even when he meets Marty, but once he is in trouble and no one helps him except Marty he changes. Marty's kindness changes him. A - Jack did not win the race. C - Marty helped Jack before he won. D - Lawrence and Jack do not become friends.
8 PART B	D	Paragraph 12 gives proof of this. (stated above) A- Jack got stuck in the thorn bush, B - Jack and Marty raced, C - Marty won the race... none of these do not give evidence that supports what changed Jack from being selfish.
9	C	Jack knew that Marty wanted to win the race to help his mother and siblings. Marty still stopped to help Jack when no one else would. This turned Jack's attitude around and he became friends with Marty from that point in the story. A - Jack was never mad at Marty, B- Jack was annoyed by Marty at the beginning of the story, D- Jack was not disappointed in Marty-he congratulated him for winning the race.
10	A	Evidence from the story shpws that Jack began to see Marty differently once he was helped unexpectedly by Marty. B - Jack just listened and looked disturbed- he did not think he was going to be friends with Marty, C-When Marty lined up to wish Jack luck, Jack was still annoyed with Marty, D-When Marty introduced himself to Jack... Jack still was too self-absorbed.
11 PART A	C	Green beans are skinny. Jack is skinny, and another word for skinny is thin. A - It did not say he was green like a green bean-but skinny like a green bean, B - Green beans are not fat, D - Green beans were not described as smelly.
11 PART B	A	Jack just flew through the brush-He was light, skinny, and thin. B and D described other attributes of Jack's appearance, but not size. C - described the rabbits Jack saw at the race.

      LumosLearning.com   ▲

Question No.	Answer	Detailed Explanation
12	C	A hyperbole is a word or phrase that is extremely exaggerated. Jack's ears are not really as tall as the Empire State Building; the author says that so you know they are really big.

Unit 2

Question No.	Answer	Detailed Explanation
13 PART A	B	A synonym for pit is holes. A and D are not a pit or hole. Stars are in the sky and hills are mounds of earth. Option C, dents, is close to the meaning- holes are the best answer according to dictionary definitions as well as the story gives the answer of holes.
13 PART B	C	It mentions the pits as holes. B and D talk about what the moon is made of, and A discusses what role gravity plays on the moon.
14 PART A	B	The story talks about Galileo making the telescope where he can see the surface of the Moon from the Earth. A and C do not support the evidence from the passage, and D is not even discussed.
14 PART B	Paragraph 5	This paragraph gives evidence on the purpose of the telescope.
15	C	Paragraph 13 explains how important that small step truly was and how it shows how far mankind will go.
16 PART A	D	A landmark is a well-known object on a piece of land.
16 PART B	A	None of those are an example of the definition of a landmark. Maps and Breadcrumbs may be found in the story but are not evidence for landmark. A landmark is a real object
17 PART A	C	On a map you would either find a picture of a landmark on the map or the map key describing what type of landmark it is. Map Title, Compass Rose, and Distance Scale are all things found on a map-Landmarks are not on these items.
17 PART B	B	The passage actually gives definitions of the parts of the map. So it describes what a map key is. A, C, and D give definitions that do not give evidence to supporting landmarks.
18	B, E, and G	Paragraph 4 lists the supporting details as to why a map is important.

Question No.	Answer	Detailed Explanation
19		See Rubric Page No. 10 & 11
	Unit 3	
20 PART A	B	Cluster means Group
20 PART B	A	For two birds it would take a group of leaves, instead of one leaf, to shelter them from the rain. It also states the leaves will protect them from the rain. B, C, and D describe the limb they sit on and the hole in the trunk but not what a cluster is.
21	A, D, and E	These tell the physical attribute of the setting (tree) and where the tree is located-which is the setting as well.
22	D	The lark made his home where his friend the sparrow lives instead of the Tundra. A is not it because the lark is not sad to move, B- The lark is not just visiting his friends, and C- it does not just talk about singing.
23	C	The poem ends by stating it is home of Cassandra the sparrow and the lark. A-just talks about it being the home of the lark, B-talks about him leaving the tundra, and D-just talks about them singing.
24	A	Line 2 describes the lark.
25		See Rubric Page No. 10 & 11
26 PART A	A	The text discusses the answer as a reason to why Henry Ford's company grew worldwide. B - Henry never went back to farming. C and D Henry Ford did do, but the Major change was A.
26 PART B	C	This detail from the story, shows why Henry Ford made assembly lines. A - supports C from question A; B - is a result of the assembly line but the best answer is A; D discusses how the assembly line started out.
27 PART A	C	The whole article revolves around the idea of how she loves her car, the appearance, sound, etc. and how she was devastated when she got into a fender bender. A and B are details for the story. D - She never wanted a new car because she loved her old one.

     LumosLearning.com   ▲

Question No.	Answer	Detailed Explanation
27 PART B	C	The narrator commented that her car deserved the best because she was the prettiest ever made. A and B are descriptions of the car. D - discusses the detail of the fender bender.
28	B	In "Boom, Crash, Bang" she drove a Mustang and Henry Ford was the creator of Ford. His creation was in a fender bender and it would have made him cry. A - Henry Ford was not the narrator's dad, C - Henry Ford was not in the car, D - The accident did not happen by Henry Ford's farm.
29	7, 7 or 9	Evidence from text to support the answer above.
30 PART A	D	Example of the Shelby Mustang in the movie *Gone in 60 Seconds.* A, B, and C were not examples in the story "Henry Ford"
30 PART B	7, 9	Evidence from text that proves the above.

Summative Assessment (SA) - 2

Student Name:
Test Date:

Start Time:
End Time:

Here are some reminders for when you are taking the Grade 3 ELA Summative Assessment (SA)

To answer the questions on the test, use the directions given in the question. If you do not know the answer to a question, skip it and go on to the next question. If time permits, you may return to questions in this session only. Do your best to answer every question.

Unit 1

Read "Ali the Alligator" and answer the questions that follow.

Ali the Alligator
by Carla Gajewskey

1. One morning Ali the Alligator woke up to a toothache. Ali went down stairs for breakfast. Her mom made her frog legs covered in worms. Ali thought that she would just take one bite. She got her fork ready, opened her mouth, and CHOMP. Ali cried with pain.

2. Her mom ran to Ali and asked her what happened. Ali cried, big alligator tears, and told her mom she would never be able to eat frog legs again because her tooth hurts.

3. Ali's mom told her that she just needed to go to the dentist. "What is a dentist?" Ali asked. Her mom told her that a dentist was someone who is a doctor for your teeth. Ali was very excited to go to the dentist so that the doctor could fix her tooth.

4. Ali and her mom went to Dr. Chewy's Swamp Smiles. She started to get nervous and held her mom's tail tight.

5. Ali felt a pat on her back and looked up to find Dr. Chewy, her dentist. His smile showed all of his nice, sharp alligator teeth.

     LumosLearning.com   ▼

6. "Wow, how do you get your teeth to look like that?" Ali asked.

"Simple," Dr. Chewy said. "You just need to follow two rules; always remember to brush and floss your teeth every night before you go to bed and every morning when you wake up. This will keep you from having cavities, which is what causes tooth aches."

7. Ali was so upset that she didn't listen to her mom when she was told to brush her teeth every night and morning.

8. Dr. Chewy told her that he would be able to fix her tooth, but she must take care of it and her other teeth. Once Dr. Chewy was finished with Ali's teeth she felt so happy, and promised that she would brush her teeth every morning and night.

9. This made Dr. Chewy smile his big gator smile, and he gave her a pretty purple tooth brush. Ali could not wait to try her new tooth brush, and eat her frog legs.

1.   **Part A**

What is the meaning of the word <u>nervous</u> as it is used in paragraph 4?

Ⓐ **Uneasy**
Ⓑ **Happy**
Ⓒ **Sad**
Ⓓ **Shy**

Part B

Which detail from the story best supports the answer to Part A?

Ⓐ **Ali cried with pain.**
Ⓑ **Ali was so upset that she didn't listen to her mom when she was told to brush her teeth every night and morning.**
Ⓒ **Ali cried, big alligator tears, and told her mom she will never be able to eat frog legs again because her tooth hurts.**
Ⓓ **She held her mom's tail tight.**

2.   **Part A**

How would you describe Dr. Chewy?

Ⓐ **Scary**
Ⓑ **Mean**
Ⓒ **Shy**
Ⓓ **Nice**

Part B

In the box below, write the letters of the two details from the story that support your answer to Part A

Ⓐ Ali felt a pat on her back and looked up to find Dr. Chewy, her dentist. His smile showed all of his nice, sharp, alligator teeth.
Ⓑ Ali and her mom went to Dr. Chewy's Swamp Smiles.
Ⓒ Ali was so upset that she didn't listen to her mom when she was told to brush her teeth every night and morning.
Ⓓ This made Dr. Chewy smile his big gator smile, and he gave her a pretty purple tooth brush.
Ⓔ Ali's mom told her that she just needed to go to the dentist.
Ⓕ Her mom told her that a dentist was someone who is a doctor for your teeth

3. After reading the statement in the box labeled EFFECT, pick the correct letter that is the cause and write it in the box labeled "CAUSE."

CAUSE		EFFECT
		Ali cried, big alligator tears.

Ⓐ This made Dr. Chewy smile his big gator smile.
Ⓑ His smile showed all of his nice, sharp alligator teeth.
Ⓒ Her mom made her frog legs covered in worms
Ⓓ She got her fork ready, opened her mouth, and CHOMP.

     LumosLearning.com   ▼

Read "Rex the Bully" and answer the questions that follow.

Rex the Bully
by Carla Gajewskey

1. Did you know it is hard being a dinosaur? Yes, we are big and scary, but there is always some-one bigger and scarier. This someone is Rex. He is a Tyrannosaurus Rex dinosaur. Everyone is scared of Rex.

2. My name is Albert. I am smaller than Rex. He makes me do his homework, takes my ice cream money, and pushes me around on the playground. Everybody just laughs at me. I do not have any friends because everyone is scared of Rex.

3. Most days I hide behind a huge tree at our playground.

4. One day when I was behind my tree I heard a tiny voice, "Your name is Albert, right?" I looked everywhere but did not see anyone. Then I heard, "Down here!" When I looked down I saw a tiny dinosaur.

5. She said her name was Sara. She was even smaller than me. We became best friends.

6. Sara asked me if I ever told anyone about Rex. I told her that I was too scared. Sara told me it is important to let your teachers and parents know when someone is being mean or a bully.

7. I told Mrs. Currie, my teacher, and she talked to the class about bullying, and how we can stop it. After that the other dinosaurs stopped laughing when Rex was mean, and Rex stopped being a bully.

8. Sara taught me something. Always tell an adult you trust when someone is bullying you.

4.   **Part A**

What is another word that means the same as <u>tiny</u> as it is used in paragraph 4?

Ⓐ Big
Ⓑ Plump
Ⓒ Small
Ⓓ Red

Part B

Which <u>two</u> details from the story best support the answer to Part A?

Ⓐ After that the other dinosaurs stopped laughing when Rex was mean, and Rex stopped being a bully.
Ⓑ She was even smaller than me.
Ⓒ Yes, we are big and scary, but there is always someone bigger and scarier.
Ⓓ We became best friends.
Ⓔ Your name is Albert, right?" I looked everywhere but did not see anyone.
Ⓕ Then I heard, "Down here!"

5.   **Part A**

Which statement best expresses one of the themes of the story?

Ⓐ It is okay to laugh when someone is being mean.
Ⓑ Always let an adult know when you are being bullied.
Ⓒ Making someone do your homework is okay.
Ⓓ You shouldn't be friends with people bigger than you.

Part B

Which detail from the story provides the best evidence for the answer to Part A?

Ⓐ Sara told Albert that it is important to let your teachers and parents know when you are being bullied.
Ⓑ Albert was smaller than Rex.
Ⓒ All of Albert's classmates laughed when Rex was mean to him.
Ⓓ Albert hid behind a big tree.

6. **Write the letter of three character traits that best fit Rex in the boxes labeled character traits.**

Ⓐ **Kind**
Ⓑ **Fun**
Ⓒ **Mean**
Ⓓ **Lazy**
Ⓔ **Honest**
Ⓕ **Thief**

```
                        ┌──────────────┐
                        │              │
                        │     REX      │
                        │              │
                        └──────────────┘
                        ╱      │       ╲
                       ╱       │        ╲
CHARACTER TRAIT    CHARACTER TRAIT    CHARACTER TRAIT
┌─────────────┐   ┌─────────────┐   ┌─────────────┐
│             │   │             │   │             │
│             │   │             │   │             │
│             │   │             │   │             │
└─────────────┘   └─────────────┘   └─────────────┘
```

7. **You have read two stories "Ali the Alligator" and "Rex the Bully". Compare and contrast the character Ali from "Ali the Alligator" to the character Rex from "Rex the Bully". Include their physical attributes, character traits, attitude, feelings, and moods.**

   Be sure to include specific details from each story to support your ideas.

```
┌────────────────────────────────────────────────────┐
│                                                      │
├────────────────────────────────────────────────────┤
│                                                      │
│                                                      │
└────────────────────────────────────────────────────┘
```

© Lumos Information Services 2016   LumosLearning.com

Read "The Big Cheese" and answer the questions that follow.

The Big Cheese
by Carla Gajewskey

1. Chester loved all kinds of cheese, but his favorite was Swiss cheese.

2. Chester was plump with big round ears, a long tail, and a button nose. Chester was a mouse. He was a very clean mouse, but a mouse nonetheless.

3. He lived in a small hole in the wall just behind the stove. It was the perfect place because no one knew he was there, and there were always good crumbs to eat.

4. The cheese was a bit more challenging to get to.. It was always on a plate placed on the counter by the sink.

5. Chester would have to scurry past Sylvia the cat. Sylvia had been trying to catch Chester for years but never had any luck.

6. Since Chester was getting older and plumper, he was worried that Sylvia would be able to catch him soon for her favorite snack, mouse.

7. Chester decided to start looking for a new place to live.

8. Ollie the Owl asked him if he ever considered moving to the moon. She said that the moon was made of cheese, blue cheese at that.

9. Chester thought on this for a moment and realized that he really didn't even know where the moon was, but blue cheese sounded close enough to Swiss cheese.

10. Ollie told him to come back once it got dark and she would show him where the moon was.

11. Chester came back at dark and waited for Ollie. Finally, Ollie came swooping down and landed on her limb.

12. Chester did not waste any time with small talk and asked Ollie where the moon was. She pointed to a huge lit up ball in the sky. Chester was stunned by how big it was and asked, "All of that is made of cheese?"

13. Chester said, "I could live off of that for a life time. How do I get up there?"

Ollie said, "I heard about those rocket things that will shoot you up to the moon."

14. Chester remembered one of the boys in the house he lived in made a bottle rocket for a science fair project. Chester knew he had to get that bottle rocket, and he needed Ollie's help.

15. He went inside and tiptoed past Sylvia to the closet of crafts. That is where he last saw the rocket.

16. Once he saw it, he motioned for Ollie to fly in from the window that had been left open in the kitchen. Ollie flew in without a sound, grabbed the bottle rocket with her feet, and flew out. Chester could not believe how quiet she was.

17. He ran to the junk drawer in the office and grabbed a few matches.

18. Chester then began to run to the cat door and ran right into Sylvia. Sylvia grabbed him, but Chester slipped out of her paws and out the cat door. Sylvia was right behind him.

19. He saw the bottle rocket in the open field. He struck the match, lit the rocket as he ran by it, and then jumped in. Chester yelled, "Come on! Come on!" The bottle rocket just fizzed, and nothing happened.

20. Chester just froze in fear as Sylvia grabbed the rocket. She held the rocket in her paws as it started sputtering. All of a sudden, she pointed it facing the moon and it took off.

21. Chester cried "Yee, Haw!" The moon got closer and closer. Finally the rocket was flying over the moon. Chester jumped off and rolled into a big hole.

22. He sat up and realized that Swiss cheese doesn't even have holes this big. He grabbed a big clump, took a bite, and smiled. Chester thought to himself, "Home is where the heart is, or at least where the cheese is!"

8. **Part A**

What character trait best describes both Chester and Sylvia?

Ⓐ **Lazy**
Ⓑ **Grumpy**
Ⓒ **Like to eat**
Ⓓ **Shy**

Part B

Choose two paragraph numbers from the above passage that support your answer to Part A and then write them in the box below.

```
┌─────────────────────────────┐
│                             │
│                             │
│                             │
└─────────────────────────────┘
```

LumosLearning.com   ▼

9.   **Part A**

What is the theme for the story the Big Cheese?

Ⓐ Sometimes we have to move to better our lives.
Ⓑ Let your stomach decide where you move.
Ⓒ The moon is made of cheese.
Ⓓ The moon is very expensive property.

Part B

Which detail from the story provides the best evidence for the answer to Part A?

Ⓐ Ollie the Owl asked him if he ever considered moving to the moon. She said that the moon was made of cheese, blue cheese at that.
Ⓑ He sat up and realized that Swiss cheese doesn't even have holes this big. He grabbed a big clump, took a bite, and smiled.
Ⓒ Since Chester is getting older and plumper he is worried that Sylvia will be able to catch him soon for her favorite snack, mouse.
Ⓓ Finally the rocket was flying over the moon. Chester jumped off and rolled into a big hole.

10.   **Part A**

What is the meaning of the word <u>scurry</u> as it is used in paragraph 5 in "The Big Cheese?"

Ⓐ Move slowly
Ⓑ Freeze
Ⓒ Dance
Ⓓ Move quickly

Part B

Which detail from the story provides the best evidence for the answer in Part A?

Ⓐ Sylvia has been trying to catch Chester for years, but never has had any luck.
Ⓑ It was the perfect place because no one knew he was there, and there was always good crumbs to eat.
Ⓒ Since Chester is getting older and plumper.
Ⓓ Chester just froze in fear as Sylvia grabbed the rocket.

11. Create a timeline of the most important events in "The Big Cheese" by writing the letters of three sentences into the boxes, in the correct order. Read carefully as some events may not be mentioned in the passage.

Ⓐ She held the rocket in her paws as it started sputtering.
Ⓑ Chester decided that it was better to be just himself.
Ⓒ Chester said, "I could live off of that for a life time. How do I get up there?"
Ⓓ Chester climbed onto a table and yelled.
Ⓔ Chester decided to start looking for a new place to live.

EVENT 1	EVENT 2	EVENT 3

12. Why was the cheese more challenging to reach?

Ⓐ Chester had to cross the entire kitchen.
Ⓑ Chester had to jump from the counter to the kitchen island.
Ⓒ Chester was a young mouse, but he only had three legs.
Ⓓ Chester was older and had to pass Sylvia the cat to reach it.

Unit 2

Read "Home Sweet Home" and answer the questions that follow.

Home Sweet Home

1. Many years ago I lived right in front of a spring fed Lake. My house was a small log cabin.

2. In the mornings I would sit out on my back porch. I would sip my coffee and watch the ripples in the lake.

3. In the afternoon I would walk to the other side of the lake where a rope swing hung. I would run, grab the rope, and swing out over the lake.

4. Once I got over the lake I would fall in. The cool water covered my body. I would swim up to the top and just float. I went swimming every day that summer. As much time as I spent in the water I never paid much attention to the huge pile of limbs, logs, and twigs in the middle of the lake.

5. One morning that was about to change. I sat on my back porch drinking my coffee, and noticed something missing. I planted a peach tree close to the lake. It was the perfect place, or that is what I thought.

6. There were three peaches on that baby peach tree. In a few days they would have been ready to eat. My mouth watered just thinking about biting into one of those juicy peaches. After what I saw that morning my mouth dried up. My peach tree was gone. Not just the peaches but the entire tree.

7. I walked out to where the peach tree was supposed to be. I tried to think to myself what could have happened. By the time I got to the tree I figured it must have been aliens of some sort. When I looked down I saw just a stub left of my peach tree. It looked as if something just chewed right through the tiny trunk.

8. I looked out towards the pile of wood in the middle of the lake and saw one of my peach limbs. I then realized that my very quiet neighbors, Mr. and Mrs. Beaver, thought my tree would make a nice addition to their home.

9. Beavers are known to be as busy as bees. They are excellent homebuilders.

10. Beavers love lake property as well. This explains why Mr. and Mrs. Beaver loved my lake. It was quiet, peaceful, and fresh from the spring.

11. If a beaver does not find a lake or pond they will make one. Beavers will make a dam by chewing down trees and branches with their teeth. They will use that and mud to block streams and turn fields and forests into large ponds.

12. Beavers construct their homes out of branches and logs. You can see the dome from the top of the water. The entrance to their home is underwater. This looked just like Mr. and Mrs. Beaver's home in the middle of the lake.

13. Beavers can hold their breath for 15 minutes. So this makes it possible to get in and out of their house.

14. Beavers build their home for themselves, their children or yearlings, and babies or kits.

15. Beavers stay with one another for their life. I'm not sure how many anniversaries Mr. and Mrs. Beaver celebrated, or how many kits they have had, but by the look of their lodge it was a lot.

16. I was not upset with my neighbors because they were trying to care for their family. The way they take care of them is by using resources they find off of the land around them.

17. How can I fault them for having good taste? I would have chosen the best tree for my home too.

13.   **Part A**

What is the meaning of the word <u>construct</u> as it is used in Paragraph 12?

Ⓐ **Look**
Ⓑ **Destroy**
Ⓒ **Love**
Ⓓ **Build**

Part B

Which detail from the story supports the answer to Part A?

Ⓐ **How can I fault them for having good taste? I would have chosen the best tree for my home too.**
Ⓑ **Beavers are known to be as busy as bees. They are excellent homebuilders.**
Ⓒ **You can see the dome from the top of the water.**
Ⓓ **Beavers can hold their breath for 15 minutes.**

14. **Part A**

What will happen if a Beaver cannot find a lake or pond to live in?

Ⓐ They will make one.
Ⓑ They will keep looking until they find one.
Ⓒ They will learn to live on the land.
Ⓓ They will cut down your peach tree anyway.

Part B

Write the number of the paragraph in the box that gives supporting details to the answer from Part A.

Supporting Details [   ]

15. In paragraph 8, how did the author realize who had used his peach tree?

Ⓐ He saw the beavers.
Ⓑ He saw the peaches floating.
Ⓒ He saw the tree limb.
Ⓓ He saw a new house being built.

Read "Who is Albert?" and answer the questions that follow.

Who is Albert?
by Carla Gajewskey

1. I am sure you have heard about Rex, who was one mean dinosaur, but did you ever hear about Albert? He was pretty mean too.

2. Albertosaurus dinosaur bones were found in Canada by Barnum Brown. He put these bones in a basement for many years.

3. Philip Currie wanted to know more about this dinosaur. He started digging for answers to his questions.

4. He found that this dinosaur did not eat plants, but was a meat eater.

5. He had many sharp teeth, and could crush bones with his strong jaw.

6. He also could smell and see very well.

7. The Tyrannosaurus rex was part of his family. He was not as big as Rex, but he was still strong.

8. The bones of twenty-two Albertosaurus dinosaurs were found in one spot.

9. What did this mean? Did the Albertosaurus live in groups, hunt together, and even die together. This is a good guess since other meat eating dinosaurs have been found in groups.

10. You can find many clues to the past by digging in the ground.

11. The items you find will let you know who or what lived here before you.

12. When you go home dig deep. You may find that army man toy you have been looking for, or maybe your doll's shoe. You might find shells, or neat rocks. Who knows, you might even find a dinosaur bone in your backyard.

16.   Part A

What is the meaning of the word <u>crush</u> as it is used in paragraph 5?

Ⓐ **To eat**
Ⓑ **To build**
Ⓒ **To break into small pieces**
Ⓓ **To become sad**

          LumosLearning.com   ▼

Part B

Which detail from the story best supports the answer to Part A?

Ⓐ Albertosaurus dinosaur bones were found in Canada by Barnum Brown.
Ⓑ The Albertosaurus had many sharp teeth and a strong jaw.
Ⓒ He could see and smell well.
Ⓓ He was a meat eater.

17. **Part A**

A <u>carnivore</u> is an animal that eats meat, and an <u>herbivore</u> is an animal that eats plants. Which of the following was the Albertosaurus? Write either carnivore or herbivore in the box below.

CARNIVORE OR HERBIVORE

Part B

Write the number from two paragraphs that support your answer from Part A.

Support One

Support Two

18. Archeologists are scientists who dig and find things in the ground to study. According to the passage, what sorts of things can they find?

Ⓐ They might find shells, or neat rocks.
Ⓑ They might find a live dinosaur.
Ⓒ They might find the different types of grass in your yard.
Ⓓ They might find a map to a buried treasure.

19. In the story "Home Sweet Home" the author describes the characteristics of the beaver and his shelter. Think of another animal, of your choosing. Compare and Contrast the characteristics of that animal and his shelter to the characteristics of the beaver and his shelter. Be sure to use specific details from "Home Sweet Home" in your writing.

LumosLearning.com

Unit 3

Read "Just Try One More Time" and answer the questions that follow.

Just Try One More Time
by Carla Gajewskey

1. Itchy tulle, bright make-up, tap shoes, and more. Katie loved going to dance class.

2. She wore a pink leotard, pink tights, a pink tutu, and pink ballet shoes. It is a good thing Katie's favorite color was pink.

3. Her teacher, Ms. Anna, danced in many ballets, and loved Katie's class most of all.

4. Katie was a superstar at turns and leaps. She didn't even have to practice.

5. One day Ms. Anna was ready to teach them something new. Katie could not wait to find out what it was.

6. Ms. Anna told her students about the importance of flexibility in dance. She went on to slide her front foot forward and her other foot backward all the way to the floor. Ms. Anna told the students that this was a front split, and before the students could do this they would have to work on their stretches.

7. Katie knew she could do this, and started to do a front split. She was not even half way to the ground when pain rushed up both her legs. Katie quickly got up. She looked at Ms. Anna confused. Ms. Anna said, "There are things in life that we do not get the first time. These are the things that we must practice and work on until we get them."

8. Katie worked on her stretches every day. She would get closer and closer to the floor, but never made it all the way.

9. One day Katie just got up, sat on her tape, and cried. Ms. Anna walked over and asked Katie what was wrong.

10. Katie said, "I will never get this! I have practiced and practiced and it still hurts! I give up!"

11. Ms. Anna went on to explain that most people give up just when they are about to achieve success.

12. Ms. Anna told Katie her homework every night until the next practice was to think about what Thomas Edison said. He said, "The most certain way to succeed is always to try just one more time."

13. The next day Katie sat in her room and thought about this. She said to herself, "Just try one more time." Katie stretched and tried her forward split. She didn't make it all the way to the floor.

14. Katie did this every night saying to herself to try one more time, and every night she got closer but she did not make it.

15. When it was time for class they all started their stretches and with a heavy sigh Katie said, "Just try one more time." This time when she did her forward split she slid down to the floor with ease. Katie looked at Ms. Anna and they both smiled.

20.   **Part A**

What is the meaning of the word <u>flexibility</u> in paragraph 6 of *Just Try One More Time*?

Ⓐ Stiff
Ⓑ Tense
Ⓒ Soft
Ⓓ Limber

Part B

Which detail from *Just Try One More Time* uses a word that also means <u>flexibility</u> or <u>flexible</u>?

Ⓐ Achieve
Ⓑ Stretches
Ⓒ Slide
Ⓓ Try

21.   Which statement best expresses one of the themes of the story?

Ⓐ Never give up, but keep trying.
Ⓑ Always do your stretches.
Ⓒ Everyone should practice ballet.
Ⓓ Pink is the best color.

22.   Which detail from the story provides the best evidence for the answer to Question 16?

Ⓐ Katie's whole ballet outfit is pink.
Ⓑ Katie's teacher tells them that they need to practice the splits by working on their stretches.
Ⓒ Katie repeats to herself, just try one more time every night when she practices.
Ⓓ Katie loves ballet.

23. **Write the correct letter in the three empty boxes labeled character attributes. You will pick the three attributes that represent Ms. Anna.**

   Ⓐ Unkind
   Ⓑ Motivating
   Ⓒ Boring
   Ⓓ Flexible
   Ⓔ Uplifting
   Ⓕ Nervous

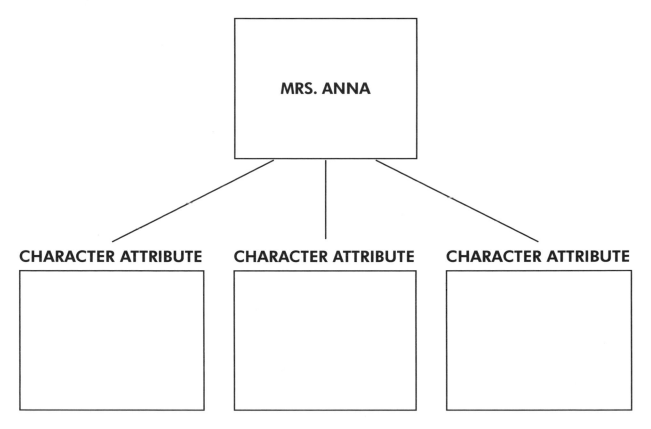

24. **How did Thomas Edison's quote, mentioned in paragraph 9 of the passage above, relate to Katie's struggles?**

   Ⓐ Katie was ready to give up and his quote told her to do it.
   Ⓑ Katie was ready to give up and his quote told her not to.
   Ⓒ Kate was ready to give up but her teacher told her not to.
   Ⓓ Katie gave up on dancing just like Edison did.

Narrative

25.   What has been your greatest accomplishment and what did you do to get there?

© Lumos Information Services 2016   LumosLearning.com   ▼

Read "Healthful Sports for Boys" and answer the questions that follow.

Healthful Sports for Boys
by Alfred Rochefort
Adapted by Marisa Adams

1. Spring winds favor kite flying. This is another world-wide sport. During the time when Egyptians were making pyramids, it was popular with old and young in China which is known as the land of the kite.

2. Many know that the great Ben Franklin learned about lightning through a kite and went on to invent electricity. But, the kite is a model that is not seen anymore. This was the old bow kite, the kind that every beginner use to make.

THE HEXAGONAL KITE

3. The hexagonal, or six sided, kite works better than the old sort. It is quite as cheap and as easily made. And kites like these have been used for more than just flying. They have been used to get a line from a stranded boat to the shore. Engineers have also used them. They did it when the first suspension bridge was built at Niagara Falls in New York. Kites have also been used to pull light vehicles over smooth ground, and they make good sport when made to pull sleds over the ice.

THE STAR KITE

4. The Star Kite is easily made and it is worth the time to learn how to do it. Get three sticks and make sure they are equal. These are joined in the center, so that they will form a six-pointed star. The covering should be thin, cotton cloth, or, better still, a light, strong paper. It must be glued so it will not be blown off. The tail band is made with a simple loop joined to the sticks at the bottom so that it will hang below the kite. The tail will balance the kite when it flies.

THE BARREL KITE

5. The barrel kite, which is specifically American, cannot be ignored. This kite was tried some years ago by the U. S. Weather Bureau officers in California. The kite looks like a long can. It is about four feet long, and two feet in diameter. The frame is made up of four light hoops. These circles are stuck together by four or more thin strips of wood. The twelve-inch space between the pair of hoops at either end is covered with paper. Then the string, which attaches the kite to a stick, is passed diagonally through the inside of the cylinder from one end to the other. When this kite catches the wind it lifts quickly and gracefully.

KITE MESSENGERS

6. Children often find fun in sending "messengers" up the strings to the kites. To do this, after the kite is high in the sky, cut round pieces of colored paper. Make a hole in the center of each circle and slip them on the string. They travel with the speed of the wind till they reach the kite, where they stop. If too heavy, or too many, the messengers may get the kite out of balance.

A messenger has been sent up 6,000 feet, or over one mile. That is the height to which American scientists have sent kites with thermometers and barometers attached, so as to record the elevation and the temperature.

26.   **Part A**

What does the word <u>messengers</u> mean as it is used in paragraph 6?

Ⓐ **writing letters to loved ones and sending them through the air**
Ⓑ **sending mail to friends and family by kite**
Ⓒ **sending round pieces of colored paper up the kite**
Ⓓ **sending messages to friends flying kites with you.**

Part B

Which answer gives evidence to the above answer?

Ⓐ **Children often find fun in sending "messengers".**
Ⓑ **If too heavy, or too many, the messengers may get the kite out of balance.**
Ⓒ **Cut round pieces of colored paper. Make a hole in the center of each circle and slip them on the string. They travel with the speed of the wind till they reach the kite, where they stop.**
Ⓓ **That is the height to which American scientists have sent kites with thermometers and barometers attached, so as to record the elevation and the temperature.**

        LumosLearning.com   ▼

27. **Part A**

Select the letter of the correct effect that goes with the cause written in box. Write that letter in the EFFECT box.

Ⓐ The creation of Barrel Kites and Star Kites
Ⓑ Electricity and the readings of elevation and temperature.
Ⓒ Teaching children to make kite messengers
Ⓓ Creating a world-wide sport

CAUSE

The invention of kites have helped with the progression of...

EFFECT

Part B

Write the two paragraph numbers in the below box that best support your answer to Part A.

28. **Part A**

What is the main idea of paragraph 3-hexagonal kites?

Ⓐ A hexagonal kite works better than the old sort.
Ⓑ The hexagonal kite has been used for more than just flying.
Ⓒ Hexagonal kites are fun to pull sleds over the ice.
Ⓓ Hexagonal kites are six sided kites that have been used for more than just flying.

Part B

Write the 3 letters of the three details that support Part A.

Ⓐ They have been used to get a line from a stranded boat to the shore.
Ⓑ These kites have also been used to pull light vehicles over smooth ground.
Ⓒ These are joined in the center, so that they will form a six-pointed star.
Ⓓ This kite was tried some years ago by the U. S. Weather Bureau officers in California.
Ⓔ They also make a good sport when made to pull sleds over the ice.
Ⓕ Children often find fun in sending "messengers" up the strings to the kites.

29. Which kite did the author feel was important to mention, just because it was an American kite?

Ⓐ The hexagonal kite
Ⓑ The barrel kite
Ⓒ The star kite
Ⓓ The bow kite

30. Hexagonal kites are important because they have been used

Ⓐ to create electricity.
Ⓑ to take temperatures and record them for science.
Ⓒ to aid engineers in building bridges.
Ⓓ to help children have fun while learning.

End of Summative Assessment (SA) - 2

         LumosLearning.com

Summative Assessment (SA) - 2

Answer Key

Question No.	Answer	Related Lumos Online Workbook	CCSS
Unit 1			
1 PART A	A	Figurative Language Expressions	RL.3.4
1 PART B	D	Figurative Language Expressions	RL.3.4
2 PART A	D	Calling All Characters; A Chain of Events	RL.3.3
2 PART B	A and D	Calling All Characters; A Chain of Events	RL.3.3
3	D	Calling All Characters; A Chain of Events	RL.3.3
4 PART A	C	Figurative Language Expressions	RL.3.4
4 PART B	B and E	Figurative Language Expressions	RL.3.4
5 PART A	B	Tell Me Again...; Caring Characters & Life's Lessons	RL.3.2
5 PART B	A	Tell Me Again...; Caring Characters & Life's Lessons	RL.3.2
6	C, D, and F	Calling All Characters; A Chain of Events	RL.3.3
7	*	Lets Talk!	W.3.3
8 PART A	C	Calling All Characters; A Chain of Events	RL.3.3
8 PART B	Sylvia – paragraph 6; Chester – paragraphs' 9, 13, and 22	Calling All Characters; A Chain of Events	RL.3.3
9 PART A	A	Tell Me Again...; Caring Characters & Life's Lessons	RL.3.2
9 PART B	C	Tell Me Again...; Caring Characters & Life's Lessons	RL.3.2
10 PART A	D	The Context Clue Crew; Same Name, Different Game; The Roots and Affix Institute	L.3.4
10 PART B	A	The Context Clue Crew; Same Name, Different Game; The Roots and Affix Institute	L.3.4

* See detailed explanation

Question No.	Answer	Related Lumos Online Workbook	CCSS
11	E, C, and A	The Question Session	RL.3.1
12	D	The Question Session	RL.3.1
Unit 2			
13 PART A	D	Educational Expressions	RI.3.4
13 PART B	B	Educational Expressions	RI.3.4
14 PART A	A		RI.3.1
14 PART B	Paragraph 11		RI.3.1
15	C		RI.3.1
16 PART A	C	Educational Expressions	RI.3.4
16 PART B	B	Educational Expressions	RI.3.4
17 PART A	Carnivore		RI.3.1
17 PART B	Paragraphs 4 and 9	The Main Idea Arena	RI.3.2
18	A		RI.3.1
19	*	Make Your Ideas Clearer; Connecting Ideas	W.3.2
Unit 3			
20 PART A	D	Figurative Language Expressions	RL.3.4
20 PART B	B	Figurative Language Expressions	RL.3.4
21	A	Tell Me Again...; Caring Characters & Life's Lessons	RL.3.2
22	C	Tell Me Again...; Caring Characters & Life's Lessons	RL.3.2
23	B, D, and E	Calling All Characters; A Chain of Events	RL.3.3
24	B	Parts of One Whole	RL.3.5
25	*	Lets Talk!	W.3.3
26 PART A	C	The Context Clue Crew; Same Name, Different Game; The Roots and Affix Institute	L.3.4
26 PART B	C	The Context Clue Crew; Same Name, Different Game; The Roots and Affix Institute	L.3.4
27 PART A	B	Educational Expressions	RI.3.4
27 PART B	Paragraphs 2 and 6	Educational Expressions	RI.3.4

* See detailed explanation

LumosLearning.com

Question No.	Answer	Related Lumos Online Workbook	CCSS
28 PART A	D	The Main Idea Arena	RI.3.2
28 PART B	A, B, and E	The Main Idea Arena	RI.3.2
29	B	The Main Idea Arena	RI.3.2
30	C		RI.3.1

Summative Assessment (SA) - 2

Detailed Explanations

Question No.	Answer	Detailed Explanation
		Unit 1
1 PART A	A	Uneasy means the same as nervous. The others are incorrect because B, happy, is a feeling of joy; C, sad, is a feeling of being upset; and D, shy, is feeling of being reserved
1 PART B	D	This is a characteristic of being nervous/uneasy. The others are incorrect because A would support a shocked feeling, B and C would support a sad feeling.
2 PART A	D	Throughout the story, the author gave many clues that he was nice.
2 PART B	A and D	Both are two examples that show he is nice; patting her on the back, smiling, and giving her a toothbrush.
3	D	Because she had a cavity, her tooth hurt when she bit down on her frog legs.
4 PART A	C	A synonym for tiny is small. A and B are the opposite of tiny. D is a color not a size
4 PART B	B and E	The clues are he had to look down to see her, and he mentioned that she was smaller than him. The others are incorrect because A and D are not clues for size, and C is a clue for the opposite of tiny
5 PART A	B	The passage talked about how this child dinosaur was bullied and gave examples, how he felt, etc. This problem was resolved by this student telling his teacher. Options A, C, and D are the opposite of what the theme of the story is.
5 PART B	A	His new friend he made gave him the confidence to tell their teacher. She was his friend and he trusted her. B and D are not supporting evidence to the theme, just details in the story. C is a detail of being bullied but not what you should do when being bullied.

▼

Question No.	Answer	Detailed Explanation
6	C, D, and F	Mean-Rex pushed Albert around bullied him Lazy-Rex made Albert do his homework Thief-Rex would take Albert's lunch money. A, B, E are the opposite of Rex
7		See Rubric Page No. 10 & 11
8 PART A	C	Chester and Sylvia are hungry, so food drives their choices and decisions. Sylvia is always trying to catch Chester, and Chester is always looking for food (which describes how they are not lazy.) The story did not mention that either were grouchy. And, Chester talks to several people while looking for a new place to live, while Sylvia is very outgoing when it comes to capturing Chester, so they are not shy.
8 PART B	Sylvia – paragraph 6; Chester – paragraphs' 9, 13, and 22	Answers may vary, but should include some combination of these paragraphs.
9 PART A	A	Chester is getting older and will not be able to outrun Sylvia. He wants to move to a safer place. B and C are more of a literal meaning of the story, but the theme is more than that. D is not in the story.
9 PART B	C	This is the evidence that explains the answer to the question above. A, B, D are details in the story, but C actually gives a clue that Chester needed to move to better his life.
10 PART A	D	When you scurry, you move quickly. "Move slowly" is the opposite of scurry. You don't move at all when you freeze. "Dance" does not mean scurry.
10 PART B	A	Chester has to scurry or move quickly to never have been caught by Sylvia yet. B and D are just details from the story. D supports the wrong answer.
11	E, C, and A	This is the order these three events occurred in the story. Options B and D did not occur in the passage.
12	D	Chester was getting older and he was worried about Sylvia the cat catching him as she made the longer journey to the cheese.

Question No.	Answer	Detailed Explanation
		Unit 2
13 PART A	D	Although this evidence is not in the traditional location of clues around the word. It is still a major clue. If Beavers are excellent homebuilders then when they are constructing their homes, they are building them. The others are incorrect because A and D are details from the story that are not describing building or constructing; and, D is about Beavers holding their breath not building or constructing their home.
13 PART B	B	The answer is found in paragraph 9. A, C, and D are in the story but do not support the answer
14 PART A	A	This is stated directly in the passage
14 PART B	Paragraph 11	Paragraph 11 is where the answer to PART A is.
15	C	Paragraph 8 says he saw the peach tree limb sticking out of the water.
16 PART A	C	To crush something is to break it into small pieces.
16 PART B	B	The clue 'sharp teeth and jaw' helps the reader get a picture of what happens to the bone when the dinosaur bites into it. He crushes it or breaks it into small pieces.
17 PART A	Carnivore	Clues from the passage prove that the Albertosaurus is a carnivore, or meat eater.
17 PART B	Paragraphs 4 and 9	These two paragraphs are the evidence that discusses that the Albertosaurus in a meat eater.
18	A	Paragraph 8 lists some of the different items that can be found when digging.
19		See Rubric Page No. 10 & 11
		Unit 3
20 PART A	D	Another word for flexible is limber. The others are incorrect because A and B are the opposite of flexibility and C does not mean flexible.
20 PART B	B	The instructor speaks of stretches to increase flexibility. You have to be flexible to do many of the complicated stretches that dancers do. A, C, and D are not synonyms for flexible.

LumosLearning.com

Question No.	Answer	Detailed Explanation
21	A	This whole story screams to keep trying and don't give up. Even though she broke down and cried she continued to say just more time. The others are incorrect because C and D are opinions and B, the story discussed more than stretches
22	C	She repeats to herself "just one more time". A, B, and D support the answers that are not the theme of the story.
23	B, D, and E	Ms. Anna was motivating and uplifting as she sat down with Katie and gave her words of encouragement. She was flexible as she demonstrated how to do a front split.
24	B	Thomas Edison's quote encouraged Katie not to give up.
25		See Rubric Page No. 10 & 11
26 PART A	C	The definition is found in paragraph 6.
26 PART B	C	Describes what a messenger is. A, B, D are not in that paragraph and do not describe what a kite messenger is.
27 PART A	B	Option B is what helped society progress. A, C, and D are fun facts about kites but did not help with progression of society.
27 PART B	Paragraphs 2 and 6	These two paragraphs discussed where kites helped with the progression of society.
28 PART A	D	It is the main idea of the passage. The remaining choices are details about the hexagonal kites but not the main idea.
28 PART B	A, B, and E	These are all details that support the main idea. C is a detail for Star Kites. D is a detail for Barrel Kites, and F is a detail for Messenger Kites.
29	B	Paragraph 5 begins with saying the Barrel Kite cannot be ignored because it is American.
30	C	Paragraph 3 describes how this kite was used to build a suspension bridge at Niagra Falls in New York.

Practice Section

In this section, you will see additional passages and practice questions.

Practice: Literary Text

Read "Spotty the Fire Dog" and answer the questions that follow.

Spotty the Fire Dog
by Carla Gajewskey

1. Spotty is my name, and putting out fires is my game. I'm a full blooded, bad to the bone, scared of nothing, Dalmatian dog.

2. I have the best job a dog could ask for, I help Lucky County Fire Department not only put out fires but help out in disaster areas too.

3. Sometimes, I even have to assist a cat out of a tree. Cats will tell you that they are smarter than dogs, but have you ever seen a dog stuck in a tree? Case closed.

4. I work with the best and the bravest firefighters. They are real life heroes. Superman does not hold a candle to what they do. They risk their lives to save people from fires and disasters caused from hurricanes, floods, tornados and more.

5. WHOOOOOOOO! That is the sirens on the big, red fire engine. It looks like we are off on another rescue mission.

6. Hop on and ride with me. My seat is on the back of the truck. The truck goes so fast that the wind almost blows the hair right off of my head.

7. We have to get there before anyone gets hurt. My keen nose can smell up to many miles which can help the fire fighters when they are searching for people or items lost in the ruble of a disaster.

8. I can smell smoke right now. It smells like we are going to East Fifth Street where my friend Dotty and her pups live. I hope that they are okay. I just met with them last week and gave a lesson on fire safety.

9. I see smoke pouring out of the windows of Dotty's house, and three white and black spotted puppies with Dotty standing on the side of the street. Let's go check on them.

10. "Spotty! We did what you said," cried the three spotted pups. Pickles jumped around nervously and said, "We woke up to our smoke alarm going off in the kitchen.

11. "Patch was baking her famous peanut butter, chocolate chip dog bones and fell asleep. The smoke alarm went off and woke up all of us.

12. "The kitchen was filled with smoke and fire.

13. "We used our fire escape map, and we checked the door knobs to make sure they were safe. They were not hot so we knew that there was not a fire behind the door.

14. "Toby's bat dog pajama top caught on fire and he stopped running, dropped to the ground, and rolled all around to put the fire out without getting burned."

15. Dotty looked at Spotty and said, "My hero!"

16. There you go friends! All in a day's work. Oh No! I have to go. Scat the cat is stuck in the big oak tree on Fortieth again. I told you cats are not smarter than dogs.

1.   Part A

Spotty can best be described as?

Ⓐ **Loyal**
Ⓑ **Fearless**
Ⓒ **Sad**
Ⓓ **Mean**

Part B

In the box below, write the letters of the three characteristics from the story that support Part A.

Ⓐ **Bad to the bone**
Ⓑ **Dotty looked at Spotty and said, "My hero!"**
Ⓒ **My keen nose can smell up to many miles**
Ⓓ **I told you cats are not smarter than dogs.**
Ⓔ **Pickles jumped around nervously**
Ⓕ **Scared of nothing, Dalmatian dog.**

Characteristics [   ]

2.   Part A

What word best describes how the puppies were feeling after the fire?

Ⓐ **Sad**
Ⓑ **Angry**
Ⓒ **Excited**
Ⓓ **Shy**

Part B

Which detail from the story best supports the answer to Part A?

Ⓐ I hope that they are okay.
Ⓑ Patch was baking her famous peanut butter, chocolate chip dog bones and fell asleep.
Ⓒ "Spotty! We did what you said," cried the three spotted pups.
Ⓓ "We woke up to our smoke alarm going off in the kitchen."

3. Spotty describes the firefighters he works with as "heroes." Which description below describes people who are heroes?

Ⓐ Someone who is fearless while helping others.
Ⓑ Someone who is scared.
Ⓒ Someone who is a bully.
Ⓓ Someone who is lazy.

4. Which detail from the story best supports the answer to Question 8?

Ⓐ Cats will tell you that they are smarter than dogs, but have you ever seen a dog stuck in a tree?
Ⓑ "Spotty! We did what you said," cried the three spotted pups.
Ⓒ They risk their lives to save people from fires and disasters caused from hurricanes, floods, tornados and more.
Ⓓ My seat is on the back of the truck. The truck goes so fast that the wind almost blows the hair right off of my head.

5. What is the meaning of the word <u>keen</u> as it is used in paragraph 7 of the story?

Ⓐ descriptive
Ⓑ sharp
Ⓒ beautiful
Ⓓ bold

LumosLearning.com

Read "Special Gifts" and answer the questions that follow.

Special Gifts
Author Unknown

1. Sonya's grandmother was her best friend. Her parents were very busy. They loved Sonya and wanted to be with her, but they each worked two jobs just to bring in enough money for the family to manage. Sonya's grandmother had lived with the family since the day Sonya was born. She doted on Sonya, supplying her with affection and treats, stories and fun. One of their favorite activities when Sonya was just a toddler was to walk around the neighborhood, naming all the flowers.

2. "That one's a marigold," Grandma would say.

"Maygol," Sonya would repeat in her toddler way.

"And that one is a sunflower."

"Sunfowa."

"That's right," Grandma would praise.

3. As Sonya grew older, they stopped naming flowers, but they still spent a lot of time together. Grandma was the one who took Sonya to school and picked her up in the afternoon. She even volunteered in her classroom. Sonya remembered a day when she was in third grade. Grandma had taken her to the science museum. They had watched a balloon that seemed to be stuck in mid-air above a little vent. Sonya couldn't understand why the balloon didn't go up or down. Grandma explained that the vent let out hot air; heat rises, so the air carried the balloon upward. But gravity pulls things down, so the balloon was tugged downward. The two forces were in equilibrium, so the balloon stayed in one place.

4. Now that Sonya was in fifth grade, things had changed. Grandma was getting older, and slowing down. Sonya's parents also had more time at home, so Grandma didn't need to do as much for Sonya. And Sonya was changing, too. She spent more time at friends' houses, and less time with her family.

5. One day Sonya heard shocking news. Her mother told her that Grandma was in the hospital. She had fallen and broken her hip. Sonya immediately went with her parents to the hospital. They peeked in Grandma's room but she was asleep. Grandma looked frail and very old. Sonya felt scared and nervous. She wasn't sure what to do or say. Her Grandma suddenly seemed like a stranger to her.

6. The family went to the hospital entry lobby to wait for Grandma to wake up. It had a cafeteria, some comfortable seats a television, and a gift shop. As soon as Sonya saw the gift shop, she knew what she wanted. She bought some flowers and a bunch of balloons from the shop and raced back up the stairs. Grandma was sitting up.

7. "Grandma!" Sonya said. "I'm so glad you're awake. Here, I brought these for you. I chose them because –"

"I know, dear," her Grandma said.

6. **Part A**

In the box below place the letter to the best answer that would finish Sonya's comment to her Grandmother in section 7 of the passage.

Ⓐ I know you love flowers.
Ⓑ Marigolds are known to make bones heal faster.
Ⓒ Flowers smell so nice.
Ⓓ One of my favorite memories was when we use to go walking and name the flowers when I was little.

"Grandma!" Sonya said. "I'm so glad you're awake. Here, I brought these for you. I chose them because –"

Part B

Which detail from the story provides the best evidence for the answer to Part A?

Ⓐ One of their favorite activities when Sonya was just a toddler was to walk around the neighborhood, naming all the flowers.
Ⓑ She bought some flowers and a bunch of balloons from the shop.
Ⓒ Grandma had taken her to the science museum. They had watched a balloon that seemed to be stuck in mid-air above a little vent.
Ⓓ Sonya's grandmother was her best friend.

7.   **Part A**

What character trait does not describe Grandma from the passage *Special Gifts?*

Ⓐ Smart
Ⓑ Playful
Ⓒ Lazy
Ⓓ Elderly

Part B

What detail from the story gives evidence that helps prove the answer to Part A?

Ⓐ One of their favorite activities when Sonya was just a toddler was to walk around the neighborhood, naming all the flowers.
Ⓑ Grandma was the one who took Sonya to school and picked her up in the afternoon.
Ⓒ She even volunteered in her classroom.
Ⓓ All of the above

8.   **Part A**

What is the meaning of the word <u>frail</u> as used in section 5 of the passage?

Ⓐ Strong
Ⓑ Frilly
Ⓒ Delicate
Ⓓ Sturdy

Part B

Which detail from the story best supports the answer to Part A?

Ⓐ One of their favorite activities when Sonya was just a toddler was to walk around the neighborhood, naming all the flowers.
Ⓑ Sonya's parents also had more time at home, so Grandma didn't need to do as much for Sonya.
Ⓒ Grandma had taken her to the science museum.
Ⓓ She had fallen and broken her hip.

9. Why did Sonya's grandmother say, "I know" when she was given the flowers?

Ⓐ Flowers had special meaning to Sonya and her grandmother.
Ⓑ She didn't like the flowers but didn't want to hurt Sonya's feelings.
Ⓒ She was too tired to listen to Sonya's explanation.
Ⓓ Flowers were no longer her favorite things to receive as gifts.

10. Why did Sonya and her grandmother spend less time together?

Ⓐ Sonya got mad at her grandmother.
Ⓑ Sonya did not like the way her grandmother handled things.
Ⓒ Sonya spent more time with her parents and changed some.
Ⓓ Sonya no longer found her grandmother cool enough to hang out with.

Read "Sir Philip was Confused" and answer the questions that follow.

Sir Philip was Confused
Author Unknown

1. King Mortimer had sent Sir Philip into the wilderness with instructions to destroy the dragon that had been terrorizing the countryside.

2. The King had more than 500 knights, but he had chosen Sir Philip and he did not stop to explain why. King Mortimer viewed dragons as the worst menace in the kingdom.

3. When Sir Philip had first set out on his quest, he was filled with a sense of anticipation of the events to come. In his imagination, he could see what was going to happen. He would slay the dragon and receive the congratulations of King Mortimer.

4. But things didn't quite turn out that way.

5. The previous evening, Sir Philip had arrived near the lake where the dragon was supposed to live. He camped for the night, sharpened his sword, and went to bed early. In the morning, Sir Philip opened his eyes. A pair of eyes was looking into his. Large eyes. Orange eyes. Dragon eyes.

6. Sir Philip jumped out of his sleeping blankets in a great hurry, knocking over his sword. It made a great clattering noise. He chased after it. His heart was pounding with fear. He could almost feel the flames shooting from the dragon's mouth to roast him alive. Standing there, he suddenly recognized that he didn't feel very roasted, or even hot. In fact, he felt quite cold. Looking down, he figured out why. He wasn't wearing any pants.

7. "Chilly?" asked the dragon.

"Wh—what?" asked Sir Philip, shivering.

"I suppose you've come to slay me," said the dragon.

"Well, yes, I have," said Sir Philip.

"How tiresome," said the dragon. "Once every few months, some king or other sends a knight out here to try to slay me. Gets kinda boring, if you ask me. Don't you people have anything better to do?"

8. "You've been terrorizing the countryside!" said Sir Philip.

"Baloney," said the dragon.

"You eat the people's sheep," said Sir Philip.

The dragon laughed. "I'm a vegetarian," he said. "Mostly I like ferns."

"But haven't you been scaring the people?"

"People get scared when they see me, I suppose," said the dragon. "But that's just because I'm big."

"And you shoot fire out of your mouth," Sir Philip pointed out.

"A bad habit," admitted the dragon. "But I've never harmed anyone."

9. Sir Philip looked confused. "But what happens now? I have a reputation. If I come home without slaying you, no one will respect me."

"So people will only respect you if you do some killing first?" asked the dragon.

Sir Philip looked worried. "I guess you're right. But what am I supposed to do now?"

"I suggest you start by putting your pants on," said the dragon.

11. **Write one letter from the list below in each box that would be a supporting detail to the main idea.**

Ⓐ **King Mortimer had sent Sir Philip into the wilderness with instructions to destroy the dragon that had been terrorizing the countryside.**
Ⓑ **King Mortimer viewed dragons as the worst menace in the kingdom.**
Ⓒ **"You've been terrorizing the countryside!" said Sir Philip. "Baloney," said the dragon.**
Ⓓ **The dragon laughed. "I'm a vegetarian," he said. "Mostly I like ferns."**
Ⓔ **A pair of eyes was looking into his. Large eyes. Orange eyes. Dragon eyes.**
Ⓕ **"People get scared when they see me, I suppose," said the dragon. "But that's just because I'm big."**

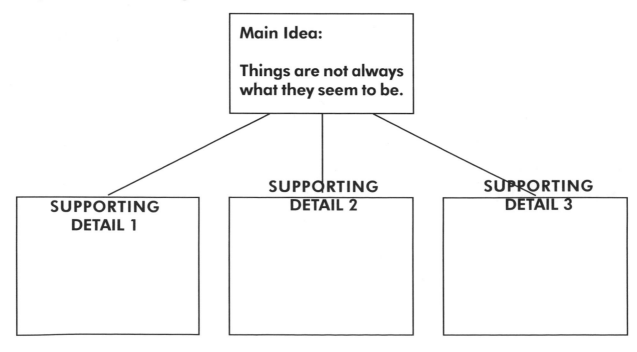

© Lumos Information Services 2016   LumosLearning.com

12. What context clue in section 1 or 2 of the passage help the reader know that <u>menace</u> means danger?

    Ⓐ Instructions
    Ⓑ Wilderness
    Ⓒ Terrorizing
    Ⓓ Destroy

13. What descriptions of the dragon help support the belief that dragons are dangerous?

    Ⓐ You eat the people's sheep; been scaring the people; And you shoot fire out of your mouth.
    Ⓑ I'm a vegetarian; I mostly like ferns; I've never harmed anyone
    Ⓒ "So people will only respect you if you do some killing first?" asked the dragon.
    Ⓓ The dragon laughed.

14. What is the meaning of the word <u>vegetarian</u> as it is used in section 8 of the passage?

    Ⓐ Sheep eater
    Ⓑ Non-meat eater
    Ⓒ Meat eater
    Ⓓ Vegetable only eater

15. What is the theme of the story, "Sir Philip's Dragon"?

    Ⓐ Always follow the directions of your king, even if you don't agree with them.
    Ⓑ Never follow the directions of your king if you do not agree with them.
    Ⓒ Always take the time to understand the people around you.
    Ⓓ Never judge a book by its cover and do not react without thinking.

Practice: Informational Text

Read "Fire Dog" and answer the questions that follow.

Fire Dog
by Carla Gajewskey

1. Dalmatian dogs go with firefighters like peas and carrots.

2. What does this white and black spotted pup do? Once upon a time, people did not have cars. Instead, they had wagons that were pulled by horses.

3. Firefighters had a fire wagon. The wagon carried everything they needed to put out a fire.

4. The Dalmatians barked in the streets when the fire wagons approached. This warned people to move out of the way for the fire wagon.

5. Dalmatians had another job. They had to keep the horses calm. Horses were known to be afraid of fire. The horses needed to bring the wagons close to the fire because the water used to put out the fires was carried in the wagon. The Dalmatians helped the horses with this.

6. Dalmatians also watched out for the fire station. They made sure no one would take the horses, the things used to put out the fire, or the fire wagon. Most fire stations had two Dalmatians. One would stay at the fire station and the other would go help put out fires. This house and wagon alarm had a bite.

7. Dalmatians are known for their hunting skills. By using their good sense of smell they would hunt the rats at the fire station. This made the firefighters happy since the rats carried germs that made them sick.

8. Even though we do not use fire wagons today, you may see a Dalmatian running out of the fire house barking. He is letting everyone know that the fire truck is leaving. You may even see him on the back of the fire truck. They like watching the fire truck while the firefighters are putting out the fire. In some cases, Dalmatians have rescued firefighters and people from fires.

9. We have come a long way from horses and wagons. Many things have changed since that time. One thing that has not changed is the Dalmatians. Their fun loving nature lives on today. They are a loyal friend to their masters. It is safe to say that the fire dog's role may be a little different, but he will always play a part in firefighting.

LumosLearning.com

16. Select the letter for the main idea and write the letter in the boxes labeled main idea. Then, choose one detail that best supports the main idea. Write the letter in the empty box labeled supporting detail.

POSSIBLE MAIN IDEAS	POSSIBLE SUPPORTING DETAILS
A. Dalmatians have played a part in helping firefighters from the past until today.	A. They had to keep the horses calm.
B. Dalmatians have a lot of energy.	B. Their fun loving nature lives on today.
C. Dalmatians are loyal	C. They are a loyal friend to their masters.
D. Dalmatians make great pets	D. It is safe to say that the fire dog's role may be a little different, but he will always play a part in irefighting.

Main Idea

Supporting Detail

17. **Part A**

Which idea is found in both the article "Spotty the Fire Dog" and "Fire Dog"?

Ⓐ Dalmatian's sense of smell helps him with his job as a Fire Dog.
Ⓑ Dalmatians warn people by barking when the fire wagons come out.
Ⓒ Dalmatians are good at calming horses.
Ⓓ Dalmatians can talk.

Part B

Choose one detail from the story "Spotty the Fire Dog" and one detail from "Fire Dog" that support the answer to Part A. Write the number of the paragraph in the correct box below.

Supporting Detail "Spotty the Fire Dog"

Supporting Detail "Fire Dog"

18.   What skill does the dalmation use in day to day life at the fire station?

    Ⓐ Smell
    Ⓑ Protecting
    Ⓒ Hunting
    Ⓓ Training

Read "What is a Cavity?" and answer the questions that follow.

What is a Cavity?
by Carla Gajewskey

1. Say cheese! It was the day of my class pictures. I smiled my big, toothless smile.

2. I just lost my front tooth the week before and got a one dollar bill from the tooth fairy.

3. I went to the store and bought the biggest candy bar a girl could buy for a dollar. My mom told me that anything sweet was not good for my teeth. Little did I know that the bacteria and plaque in our mouths love sugar and cover our teeth like ants at a picnic. Bacteria also covers our gums. Gums are the pink tissues in our mouth that hold our teeth in place. My mom told me to brush my teeth twice a day. Sometimes I did, and sometimes I didn't.

4. My mom woke me up one morning and said I had a dentist appointment. "Yay!" I squealed. I was so excited to miss a half of a day of school to go and see the dentist. All he does is clean and check my teeth.

5. In the past, I received a sticker for not having any cavities. I really did not know what a cavity was, so I decided not to worry about it. I didn't have one anyway!

6. My check up at the dentist seemed to be going very well. I was so excited that I would get a sticker for no cavities, whatever a cavity was. But then, my dentist sat down next to me and said that he wanted to go over with me how to take care of my teeth since I had a cavity. My smile faded and I looked shocked.

7. My dentist told me a cavity forms when you do not brush the bacteria away and it eats at your teeth. He also told me to brush my front teeth, back, and sides twice a day. He said to brush your teeth for at least 2-3 minutes to make sure you get all of the bacteria.

8. He said to pick out a soft bristle toothbrush every three months and showed me different types of mouthwashes and toothpastes that I could use. He then showed me how to floss by slipping the dental floss, a long thin string, between each tooth and along the gum line.

9. He said this must be done at least once a day so that I can get the bacteria out from between my teeth. He also told me that I could brush my tongue to keep my breath fresh.

10. I then said, "Wow! Taking care of teeth is hard business."

11. The dentist chuckled and said, "Only if you do not take care of your teeth. Now, let's take care of that cavity." I gave a heavy sigh and wished I would have listened to by mom.

19. What is the effect on not brushing your teeth? Write the letter to the correct answer in the box labeled **EFFECT**.

Ⓐ You will get a sticker when you go to the dentist.
Ⓑ You will get a cavity.
Ⓒ You will have good breath.
Ⓓ You will have to brush your tongue.

CAUSE

If you do not brush your teeth......

EFFECT

20. Which detail from the article help support the answer to Question 14?

Ⓐ I would always get a sticker for not having any cavities.
Ⓑ My dentist told me a cavity is when you do not brush the bacteria away and it eats at your teeth.
Ⓒ He showed me different types of mouthwashes and toothpastes that I could use.
Ⓓ He also told me that I could brush my tongue to keep my breath fresh.

21. Part A

What is the main idea of the story?

Ⓐ Floss your teeth once a day
Ⓑ Brush your teeth twice a day
Ⓒ Eat candy before bed
Ⓓ It is important to follow the appropriate steps to take care of your teeth.

LumosLearning.com

Part B

Which detail from the story does not support the answer to Part A?

Ⓐ He also told me to brush my front teeth, back, and sides as well at least twice a day.

Ⓑ He then showed me how to floss by slipping the dental floss, a long thin string, between each tooth and along the gum line.

Ⓒ My mom would tell me to brush my teeth twice a day.

Ⓓ I just lost my front tooth the week before, and got a one dollar bill from the tooth fairy.

22. **Part A**

When adding less to the word tooth it forms the word "toothless." What is the meaning of the word toothless as it is used in Paragraph 1?

Ⓐ A mouth full of teeth

Ⓑ Missing teeth

Ⓒ Dirty teeth

Ⓓ White teeth

Part B

Which detail from the story best supports the answer to Part A?

Ⓐ Gums are the pink tissues in our mouth that hold our teeth in place.

Ⓑ I just lost my front tooth the week before, and got a one dollar bill from the tooth fairy.

Ⓒ Say cheese! It was the day of my class pictures.

Ⓓ My dentist told me a cavity is when you do not brush the bacteria a way and it eats at your tooth.

23. Which word best describes the character of the dentist?

Ⓐ irritated

Ⓑ smart

Ⓒ elderly

Ⓓ friendly

Read "For the Dance" and answer the questions that follow.

For the Dance
by Carla Gajewskey

1. I sat on the soft, brown couch in Jessica Nix's living room. She was fixing us a glass of sweet iced tea. You know you are in Arkansas when you are offered sweet tea.

2. On the walls hung pictures of Jessica in her Southern Arkansas Strutter uniform. Many girls in Arkansas start dance early to prepare for the dance or drill team at the high school and college level. Jessica came back in with our sweet tea and caught me looking at her pictures.

3. *Jessica:* That picture was taken right after we won our homecoming game. I will never forget half-time. We did not make any mistakes during our show. We had so much fun.

4. *Interviewer:* How old were you when you started dance?

5. *Jessica:* I was five, and I took ballet and tap.

6. *Interviewer:* Which was your favorite?

7. *Jessica:* Tap because I loved the noise my shoes would make.

8. *Interviewer:* How did you feel the first time you were on stage?

9. *Jessica:* (Jessica laughs) I really don't remember. I think I was calm because I didn't look nervous at all on the video from recital.

10. *Interviewer:* When did dance start to become a challenge?

11. *Jessica:* It really started to become challenging when I was in junior high. I had more practices and things became harder. Of course, I made it become more challenging because I became serious about it. I became more competitive. I went from just doing dance to have fun to wanting to be good.

12. *Interviewer:* What did you do to become a better dancer?

13. *Jessica:* I stretched, stretched, stretched. That was the only way to improve my flexibility. I also practiced turns anywhere I could. My friends were on the dance team. So when we hung out we were practicing. It was fun for us.

14. *Interviewer:* How did you know you were growing into a better dancer?

15. *Jessica:* When I made All-American in the eighth grade. I was really shocked that I made it. I was the only member on the dance team that made it.

16. *Interviewer:* What does making All-American mean?

17. *Jessica:* All-American is a company that does dance camps and dance competitions. If you are noticed at these camps and competitions, you get a ribbon. Then you get to audition for various dance teams. If you make it, you get to travel. I traveled to San Antonio, Texas. Once there, I had the chance to dance with girls I didn't know. It was a great experience.

18. *Interviewer:* Who inspired you to dance?

19. *Jessica:* It was more of me wanting to do it, no matter what anyone said. I used dance as an escape from things in my life that worried me.

20. *Interviewer:* What is your favorite form of dance?

21. *Jessica:* Lyrical is my favorite form of dance because it is not as slow as ballet or as fast as jazz. The lyrical form of dance tells a story. It also is a way to release emotions through dance.

22. *Interviewer:* What advice can you give young dancers?

23. *Jessica:* My advice is to stretch, stretch, and stretch. You also need to practice a lot, but it should be fun. You can practice anywhere. No matter how hard it gets, just try one more time.

24. Jessica Nix still loves dance to this day. She has passed her love for dance to her five year old daughter Elizabeth. Elizabeth performs tap, ballet, lyrical, jazz, and participates in competitions. Jessica teaches dance and yoga in Arkansas.

24.   **What does the word <u>challenging</u> mean as it is used in paragraph 11 in the above passage?**

    Ⓐ **Healthy**
    Ⓑ **Strong**
    Ⓒ **Difficult**
    Ⓓ **Disciplined**

25.   **Part A**

    What is the theme of the interview "The Dance?"

    Ⓐ **Always stretch.**
    Ⓑ **Go to Southern Arkansas College and become a Strutter.**
    Ⓒ **Work hard at what you love.**
    Ⓓ **Lyrical dance is the best type of dance.**

Part B

Which detail from the story provides the best evidence for Part A?

Ⓐ *Jessica:* My advice is to stretch, stretch, and stretch. You also need to practice a lot, but it should be fun. You can practice anywhere. No matter how hard it gets, just try one more time.

Ⓑ On the walls hung pictures of Jessica in her Southern Arkansas Strutter uniform. Many girls in Arkansas start dance early to prepare for the dance or drill team at the high school and college level.

Ⓒ *Jessica:* Lyrical is my favorite form of dance because it is not as slow as ballet or as fast as jazz. The lyrical form of dance tells a story. It also is a way to release emotions through dance.

Ⓓ When I made All-American in the Eighth grade. I was really shocked that I made it. I was the only member on the dance team that made it.

26. In the box below write the letter of the characteristic that describes Chester from the story, "The Big Cheese" and Jessica from the Interview, "The Dance."

   Ⓐ Fear
   Ⓑ Determination
   Ⓒ Lazy
   Ⓓ Hyper

   Characteristic [   ]

Read "Washington as a Fighter" and answer the questions that follow.

WASHINGTON AS A FIGHTER
From American History Stories, Volume III
by Mara L. Pratt
Adapted by Marisa Adams

1. George Washington was known for being a quiet man. He hardly ever raised his voice and he really didn't like to fight. But, when it was needed, Washington could be loud and strong. His clear sense of right and wrong was what made him such a good General and President.

2. This event shows his strength, his firmness, and his ability to act quickly. One day, Colonel Glover's Marblehead soldiers and Morgan's Virginia Riflemen started to argue. The Virginians laughed at the way the Marbleheads talked because they had a different dialect in Marblehead, Massachusetts. The Marbleheaders, on the other hand, made fun of the way the Riflemen dressed.

3. The two groups went from yelling to hitting. Before they knew it, they were in a full fight and didn't know Washington had ridden up on his horse.

4. Washington quickly figured out what was happening. He jumped from his horse and threw the reins to his servant. Then, he ran into the middle of the fight and grabbed two of the biggest, strongest of the soldiers. He held them at arm's length and shook them until they looked at him with shock. They cried out and asked for forgiveness.

5. Then, he spoke quietly and gave directions that the two men be taken to their camps. He also said there should be no more arguing between the two groups. He rode away, leaving everyone staring in surprise at the man who was usually so peaceful.

6. Washington's actions showed his men that even though he liked peace and quiet, he could definitely act when he needed to.

27. **Part A**

Place the correct letter of the main idea of the passage "George Washington as a Fighter" in the box labeled "Main Idea".

Ⓐ Washington had a disposition of peace, but acted when necessary to make a point.
Ⓑ Washington only acted in violence.
Ⓒ Washington only used peaceful talks to solve a problem.
Ⓓ Washington spoke loudly.

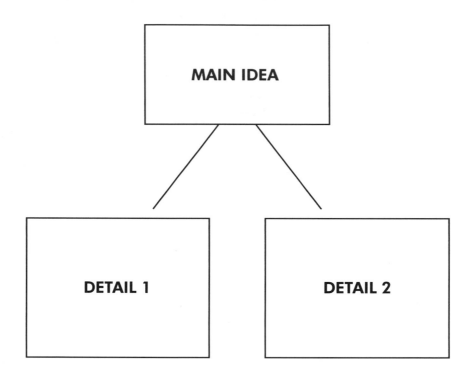

Part B

Place the two details in the three boxes above that support the main idea.

Ⓐ He hardly ever raised his voice and he really didn't like to fight. But, when it was needed, Washington could be loud and strong.
Ⓑ George Washington was known for being a quiet man.
Ⓒ Then, he spoke quietly and gave directions that the two men be taken to their camps. He also said there should be no more arguing between the two groups. He rode away, leaving everyone staring in surprise at the man usually so peaceful.
Ⓓ They cried out and asked for forgiveness.

28. **Part A**

Glover's Marblehead soldiers are called Marbleheaders in paragraph two because...

Ⓐ they wore helmets made of marble
Ⓑ their heads were round like marbles
Ⓒ they shot marbles out of their guns
Ⓓ they were from Marblehead, Massachusetts

Part B

Which statement gives evidence that the answer to Part A is correct?

Ⓐ The Marbleheaders, on the other hand, made fun of the way the riflemen dressed.
Ⓑ They had a different dialect in Marblehead, Massachusetts.
Ⓒ One day, Colonel Glover's Marblehead soldiers and Morgan's Virginia riflemen started to argue.
Ⓓ The Virginians laughed at the way the Marbleheads talked.

29. **Part A**

The dragon in the passage "Sir Philip was Confused" could be compared to George Washington, in the passage "Washington as a Fighter" because...

Ⓐ they both believe that peace should come first.
Ⓑ they both believe that fighting is the answer.
Ⓒ they both believe in holding grudges.
Ⓓ they both believe in being quiet.

Part B

Place the two letters in the Venn Diagram below that give evidence to support the answer for Part A. One letter should be chosen from the evidence of the passage "Sir Philip was Confused" and the second letter should be chosen from "Washington as a Fighter."

Passage: "Sir Philip was Confused"

Ⓐ Sir Philip looked confused. "But what happens now? I have a reputation. If I come home without slaying you, no one will respect me." "So people will only respect you if you do some killing first?" Asked the dragon.

Ⓑ When Sir Philip had first set out on his quest, he was filled with a sense of anticipation of the events to come. In his imagination, he could see what was going to happen. He would slay the dragon and receive the congratulations of King Mortimer.

Ⓒ King Mortimer had sent Sir Philip into the wilderness with instructions to destroy the dragon that had been terrorizing the countryside.

Passage:" George Washington as a Fighter"

Ⓓ He held them at arm's length and shook them until they looked at him with shock.

Ⓔ George Washington was known for being a quiet man. He hardly ever raised his voice and he really didn't like to fight. But, when it was needed, Washington could be loud and strong. His clear sense of right and wrong was what made him such a good General and President.

Ⓕ Then, he ran into the middle of the fight and grabbed two of the biggest, strongest of the soldiers.

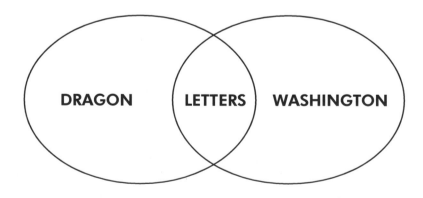

End of Practice Section

LumosLearning.com

Practice Section

Answer Key

Question No.	Answer	Related Lumos Online Workbook	CCSS
		Practice: Literary Text	
1 PART A	B	Calling All Characters; A Chain of Events	RL.3.3
1 PART B	A, B, F	Calling All Characters; A Chain of Events	RL.3.3
2 PART A	C	Calling All Characters; A Chain of Events	RL.3.3
2 PART B	C	Calling All Characters; A Chain of Events	RL.3.3
3	A	Making Words Work	L.3.5
4	C	Making Words Work	L.3.5
5	B	Same Name, Different Game	L.3.4
6 PART A	D	The Question Session	RL.3.1
6 PART B	A	The Question Session	RL.3.1
7 PART A	C	Calling All Characters; A Chain of Events	RL.3.3
7 PART B	D	Calling All Characters; A Chain of Events	RL.3.3
8 PART A	C	The Context Clue Crew; Same Name, Different Game; The Roots and Affix Institute	L.3.4
8 PART B	D	The Context Clue Crew; Same Name, Different Game; The Roots and Affix Institute	L.3.4
9	A	The Question Session	RL.3.1
10	C	The Question Session	RL.3.1
11	F, C, and D	Tell Me Again...; Caring Characters & Life's Lessons	RL.3.2
12	C	The Context Clue Crew; Same Name, Different Game; The Roots and Affix Institute	L.3.4
13	A	Calling All Characters; A Chain of Events	RL.3.3
14	B	The Context Clue Crew; Same Name, Different Game; The Roots and Affix Institute	L.3.4
15	D	Tell Me Again...; Caring Characters & Life's Lessons	RL.3.2

Question No.	Answer	Related Lumos Online Workbook	CCSS
Practice: Informational Text			
16	A, D	The Main Idea Arena	RI.3.2
17 PART A	A		RI.3.9
17 PART B	7, 7		RI.3.9
18	C		RI.3.1
19	B	Cause and Effect	RI.3.3
20	B	Cause and Effect	RI.3.3
21 PART A	D	The Main Idea Arena	RI.3.2
21 PART B	D	The Main Idea Arena	RI.3.2
22 PART A	B	The Roots and Affix Institute	L.3.4B
22 PART B	B	The Roots and Affix Institute	L.3.4B
23	D	Calling All Characters; A Chain of Events	RL.3.3
24	C	The Main Idea Arena	RI.3.2
25 PART A	C	The Main Idea Arena	RI.3.2
25 PART B	A	The Main Idea Arena	RI.3.2
26	B	Calling All Characters; A Chain of Events; Cause and Effect	RL.3.3 RI.3.3
27 PART A	A	The Main Idea Arena	RI.3.2
27 PART B	A and C	The Main Idea Arena	RI.3.2
28 PART A	D	Making Words Work	L.3.5A
28 PART B	B	Making Words Work	L.3.5A
29 PART A	A		RI.3.9
29 PART B	A and E		RI.3.9

LumosLearning.com

Practice Section

Detailed Explanations

Question No.	Answer	Detailed Explanation
		Practice: Literary Text
1 PART A	B	Throughout the passage Spotty is described us fearless.
		A - Spotty is loyal, but fearless is the best answer according to the evidence provided in the passage. C- Spotty never got sad- even when his friends were in trouble. D - Spotty was never mean but instead helpful in helping save lives.
1 PART B	A, B, F	Those are all parts from the text that give evidence that Spotty is fearless.
		C and D are characteristics but not ones that describe Fearless.
		E - Describes Pickles, not Spotty.
2 PART A	C	Part B gives evidence to this answer.
		A - The puppies were not A. sad, B. angry, or D. shy when they saw Spotty. They were excited that they were alive and followed Spotty's instructions.
2 PART B	C	Even though it was a scary event that happened to the pups and they were a little nervous they were also excited that they escaped because they did what Spotty taught them.
		A - discussed Spotty's feelings, B. discussed what Patch did to catch their house on fire, and D. explained what the puppies awoke to.
3	A	Definition of what a hero is
		Heroes - are not B. Scared, C. a bully, or D. lazy.
4	C	A part in the story actually describes what a firefighter does.
		A - talks about cats not heroes, B - discusses the puppies being excited not heroes, D - discusses where Spotty sits on the fire truck not heroes.
5	B	The meaning of the word "keen" is sharp.
		Paragraphs 7 and 8 help explain how Spotty's nose is sharp enough to smell smoke.

Question No.	Answer	Detailed Explanation
6 PART A	D	Sonya and her grandma used to walk and name flowers when she was little. A-C were not mentioned.
6 PART B	A	"Sonya and her grandma use to walk and name flowers when she was little" was discussed in the story. B, C, and D are in the story, but A is the best answer.
7 PART A	C	C, lazy, does not describe Grandma. A, B, and D are all characteristics of Grandma.
7 PART B	D	All of the answer choices are proof that Grandmother was not lazy.
8 PART A	C	Delicate is the same as frail. D and A are the opposite of frail. B means lacy
8 PART B	D	This is a clue that when grandmother broke her hip, she became frail. A-C show Grandma was not frail but strong and energetic.
9	A	Sonya did not have to say why she brought the flowers. They were so special to both of them and her Grandmother automatically knew the meaning.
10	C	The passage refers to several reasons Sonya no longer spent time with her grandmother, including the fact that Sonya's parents were home more and she was changing some.
11	F, C, and D	These options describe what or who the dragon really is - a kind dragon. Options A, B, and E make the dragon to be out mean and he really isn't.
12	C	The word terrorizing means danger. A, B, D are not clues from paragraphs 1 and 2 that help the reader figure out what menace means.
13	A	This answer gives the examples of why people believe dragons are dangerous. B-D show that the dragon is not dangerous.
14	B	Although common use of the word today means one who eats vegetables, paragraph 8 shows the Dragon does not eat sheep, or any meat; just mostly ferns which are plants. Not all plants are considered vegetables, so 'eating vegetables only' is not the correct answer.
15	D	Sir Phillip was guilty of blindly following his king's orders, but he took the time to stop and talk to the dragon. This helped him see the dragon wasn't really a danger. The purpose of the passage is to remind us to always think before acting and not just judge people based on what others say.

    LumosLearning.com   ◀

Question No.	Answer	Detailed Explanation
		Practice: Informational Text
16	A, D	The article mainly talks about how Dalmatians have helped firefighters in the past and how they help them today. One detail from the story talks about how the Dalmatian's role may be different from the past, but he still plays a part today as a fire dog. Main Idea: B, C, and D are great details about Dalmatians but not the main idea of the passage. Supporting Detail: A, B, C are details about Dalmatians but do not support the main idea of the passage.
17 PART A	A	In both articles it talks about the Dalmatian's sense of smell. A - Is only found in "Fire Dog", C - is only found in "Fire Dog", and D - is a characteristic of a fictional character in "Spotty the Fire Dog"
17 PART B	7, 7	Paragraph supporting detail for "Spotty the Fire Dog" and supporting detail for "Fire Dog".
18	C	Paragraph 7 states that dalmations use hunting skills.
19	B	The narrator got a cavity because she did not brush her teeth. A - If you do not brush your teeth you will get a cavity and not get a sticker, C - If you do not brush your teeth you will not have good breath, D - You need to brush your teeth and your tongue.
20	B	Evidence from the article proves this. A - stickers for no cavities, C - talks about what you should brush your teeth with, D talks about how to keep breath fresh-none talk about what happens when you do not brush your teeth.
21 PART A	D	The article mainly talks about the importance of taking care of your teeth. A and B are details from the passage. C - the passage never discusses eating candy before bed.
21 PART B	D	All of the answers besides D support the main idea by giving examples from the text on how to take care of your teeth. A - C are all details that support the main idea of the importance of taking care of your teeth.

Question No.	Answer	Detailed Explanation
22 PART A	B	Evidence from the second paragraph, "I just lost my front tooth the week before," helps support that toothless means missing teeth - B A, C, and D do not have evidence to support that a mouth full of teeth, dirty teeth, or white teeth would go with "less."
22 PART B	B	Evidence from the second paragraph, "I just lost my front tooth the week before," helps support that toothless means missing teeth - B A - discusses gums, not missing teeth, C - talks about smiling for pictures, D - talks about what causes a cavity.
23	D	The fact that the dentist takes the time to sit and talk to the narrator about her teeth, explain about her cavity and about the importance of taking care of her teeth, instead of simply yelling at her, shows that he is a friendly dentist.
24	C	When something is challenging, it is very difficult. Jessica had to use a lot of personal discipline to achieve her goals, but challenging does not mean discipline.
25 PART A	C	Jessica's whole story takes you down a path of working hard at what you love. A - Is just a detail from the story B - The whole story was not about Southern Arkansas College D - is an opinion
25 PART B	A	This is the answer that discusses practicing a lot, but making it fun, and to keep trying. B, C, and D were details from her life but not what the theme of the story is.
26	B	Even though one story is informational and one literary, both characters show traits of determination. Chester - to move to a safer place, made of food, and Jessica's - love for dance that made her determined to become better and practice. Option A is incorrect because both showed characteristics of being courageous not fearful. Option C is incorrect because they are both the opposite of Lazy. And, D is incorrect because it states that they were overactive or Hyper.
27 PART A	A	The story mainly talks about Washington having a disposition of peace, but of acting if needed. D- is incorrect because Washington was soft spoken. C is incorrect because Washington acted when necessary. B is incorrect because Washington mostly acted in peace.

   LumosLearning.com

Question No.	Answer	Detailed Explanation
27 PART B	A and C	These options support that he was peaceful and yet did what he needed to if it would be effective. D does not give an example to prove the main idea, and B just shows his peaceful side.
28 PART A	D	Evidence found in the story. A – C are not mentioned in the story.
28 PART B	B	That sentence comes directly from the story. A, C, and D are found in the story but do not support why the Marbleheaders are called that.
29 PART A	A	They were both peaceful. B and C are false examples of their personality. It is not stated if the dragon believes in just being quiet like Washington.
29 PART B	A and E	These are both examples of peaceful situations.

Lumos StepUp™ is an educational App that helps students learn and master grade-level skills in Math and English Language Arts.

The list of features includes:

- Learn Anywhere, Anytime!

- Grades 3-8 Mathematics and English Language Arts

- Get instant access to the Common Core State Standards

- One full-length sample practice test in all Grades and Subjects

- Full-length Practice Tests, Partial Tests and Standards-based Tests

- 2 Test Modes: Normal mode and Learning mode

- Learning Mode gives the user a step-by-step explanation if the answer is wrong

- Access to Online Workbooks

- Provides ability to directly scan QR Codes

- And it's completely FREE!

http://lumoslearning.com/a/stepup-app

lumoslearning

About Online Workbooks

- When you buy this book, 1 year access to online workbooks included

- Access them anytime from a computer with an internet connection

- Adheres to the New Common Core State Standards

- Includes progress reports

- Instant feedback and self-paced

- Ability to review incorrect answers

- Parents and Teachers can assist in student's learning by reviewing their areas of difficulty

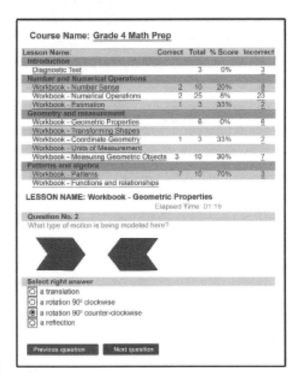

Course Name: Grade 4 Math Prep				
Lesson Name:	Correct	Total	% Score	Incorrect
Introduction				
Diagnostic Test		3	0%	3
Number and Numerical Operations				
Workbook - Number Sense	2	10	20%	8
Workbook - Numerical Operations	2	25	8%	23
Workbook - Estimation	1	3	33%	2
Geometry and measurement				
Workbook - Geometric Properties		6	0%	6
Workbook - Transforming Shapes				
Workbook - Coordinate Geometry	1	3	33%	2
Workbook - Units of Measurement				
Workbook - Measuring Geometric Objects	3	10	30%	7
Patterns and algebra				
Workbook - Patterns	7	10	70%	3
Workbook - Functions and relationships				

LESSON NAME: Workbook - Geometric Properties
Elapsed Time: 01:19

Question No. 2
What type of motion is being modeled here?

Select right answer
- a translation
- a rotation 90° clockwise
- a rotation 90° counter-clockwise
- a reflection

Previous question   Next question

Report Name: Missed Questions

Student Name: Lisa Colbright
Cours Name: Grade 4 Math Prep
Lesson Name: Diagnostic Test

The faces on a number cube are labeled with the numbers 1 through 6. What is the probability of rolling a number greater than 4?

Answer Explanation

(C) On a standard number cube, there are six possible outcomes. Of those outcomes, 2 of them are greater than 4. Thus, the probability of rolling a number greater than 4 is "2 out of 6" or 2/6.

A)		1/6
B)		1/3
C)	Correct Answer	2/6
D)		3/6

lumos learning
Developed by Expert Teachers

3
Grade

PARCC® 2017
Practice Tests
MATHEMATICS

☆ 2 Summative Assessments

★ Additional Questions by Type

(((tedBook)))

☆ Includes access to the Mobile Apps

★ Answer Key and Detailed Explanations

PLUS

ONLINE WORKBOOKS

Adheres to Common Core State Standards

www.LumosLearning.com

Available
- At Leading book stores
- Online www.LumosLearning.com

40194873R00064

Made in the USA
Middletown, DE
05 February 2017